African-American

What's Up, Dawg?

What's Up, Dawg?

How to Become a Superstar in the Music Business

RANDY JACKSON

with K. C. Baker

NEW YORK

This book is dedicated

to my mother,

Julia D. Jackson,

and my late father,

Herman C. Jackson, Sr.

Without their love and support,

I wouldn't be where I am

today and probably never

could have pulled

all this off . . .

Contents

When You Wish Upon a Star

SO YO, YOU WANNA BE A STAR, RIGHT? You want to be riding the top of the charts. You want to be cruising in limos with screaming fans jumping on the hood. You want five-star hotels. The bling bling. The hot celebrity life. You want this bad, don't you?

So let's do this.

Since I became a judge on *American Idol*, people constantly ask me about success. "My daughter has a terrific voice. How can I help her make it to the top?" "I believe I have what it takes to be a star. How do I get noticed?" "I've always wanted to be in the music business. What's the best way to get started?"

Everybody thinks it's a snap. They think it's the easiest thing in the world to be a singer. They say to me, "Yo, you know, it doesn't seem like it's really that hard. I used to sing in the choir in high school."

Oh, really, because you sang in the choir in high school, you think you've got what it takes to become a superstar? That's how delusional people can be.

As a kid, I went fishing a lot and cleaned the fish with a knife like nobody could. Does that make me a surgeon? You don't see me in the operating room. Yo, you don't see me trying to fly the space shuttle!

If that sounds ridiculous to you, well, that's the way people sound to me.

Crazy.

I see it all the time in my everyday life and especially on *American Idol*. People show up from all walks of life with absolutely no talent. They stand before me and the other two judges, Paula Abdul and Simon Cowell, and attempt to sing. And guess what? They never get through the first round. But they believe, somehow, that they've got what it takes.

I'm going to keep it real with you. No lies. No sugarcoating it. If you think you really, *truly* have what it takes to be the next Mariah Carey, Justin Timberlake, Michael Jackson, Elvis or *American Idol* winners Kelly Clarkson or Ruben Studdard, then I'll tell you how to find out if you've got "it," how to maximize whatever "itness" you may already have and how to use it to realize your dreams.

In *Idol 2*, Simon said that Keith from Atlanta was possibly the worst singer in the known world when he warbled the sorriest rendition of "Like a Virgin" we ever heard. He couldn't sing. He was tone deaf. He wouldn't know a note if somebody sent one to him. And yet he had the audacity to come and audition for what is one of the greatest talent shows ever. He was completely delusional.

Before he ever came to see us, he needed someone to keep it real with him. And so do you. I'm sure if you're reading this book, your friends and family have probably told you, "Yo, you know, you've got a dope voice. You should do something with that voice. That voice is so hot." That's the thing you hear about all the time.

Well, sorry, but you can't listen to your friends and family when it comes to this. Unless they're giving voice lessons to Christina Aguilera or Norah Jones, they're not experts in the music department. They're not going to keep it real with you. They're not going to diss you to your face and tell you that you're terrible. In fact, very few people are going to keep it real with you.

But I will.

The music industry is one of the most competitive in the world. Making it is harder than ever. Big business has taken over. It's a tough economy. Companies are not spending as much money as they used to. The music industry is in a slump.

Trying to break in? Good luck. It's harder than ever to get record companies to sign a new artist with no track record even though the business today is 50 times larger than it was in the late sixties and seventies—which I think was the most creative time in the history of music, ever. Music that we're still learning from today. Motown. Sly and the Family Stone. The Beatles. Led Zeppelin. Jimi Hendrix. Janis Joplin. Aretha Franklin. Frank Sinatra. Nat King Cole. John Coltrane. Miles Davis. Charlie Parker. Nancy Wilson. These are just some of the legends whose music exploded during this time. This is a short list of folks you want to emulate. What you want to aspire to. The greatest of the greats.

And for those of you who tune in to *American Idol*, you can see that making it on that show is no easy feat, either.

Does all this sound crazy to you? Well, it is.

But this is where I come in. I am going to help you understand how to get through this maze and realize your dreams.

The one thing that hasn't changed since the beginning of the music industry is this: Talent will take you everywhere. The record industry is always looking for new, talented people and great songs. Those are the great equalizers.

People often ask me, "Would the Beatles have made it today?" Well, yeah, because they had talent and great songs.

From my days playing neighborhood block parties in Baton Rouge, Louisiana, and out-of-the-way jazz clubs across the country to producing and writing songs on Mariah Carey's latest album, *Charmbracelet*, I know what it takes to succeed—and fail—in this business.

In my 25-plus years as a Grammy Award–winning producer, musician, performer, songwriter, record exec, manager, teacher and, of course, *American Idol* judge, I've worked on more than a thousand gold and multi-platinum albums with some of the biggest stars of our time. People like Mariah Carey, Madonna, Elton John, Celine Dion, Whitney Houston, Aretha Franklin, Bon Jovi, Billy Joel, *NSYNC and Destiny's Child.

In my career in the music business and on *Idol*, I'm responsible for trying to discover new talent, so I know first-hand, better than I've ever known, what it takes to make it big. When I played onstage and on records with Bruce Springsteen, Journey and Bob Dylan, among others, I had to learn quickly what to do—and what not to do—and it's this info I'm going to pass on to you.

In this book, I'm going to help you figure out if you have "it" and how to use it if you think you've got it. I'll tell you how to find the right teacher and what you should be learning if you want to go all the way in this business. I'll help you find your musical style and explain how it can mean the difference between scoring a record deal or not. Are you more of a 50 Cent or a Christina Aguilera?

I'll give you the lowdown on how to find a band to sing or play with and how to use the tools of the trade to make the most of your sound. I'll make suggestions on how to get your look together. You don't want to show up at an audition looking exactly like Pink or P. Diddy, but you don't want to look like a librarian, either. I'll share tricks of the trade on making a demo that the industry will pay attention to. I'll tell you how to score the all-important record deal, whether or not you should *Idol* and, most important, how to stay true to yourself.

Whether your musical style is hip-hop, rock, pop, country, alternative or any other type of music, these suggestions apply to you if you want to become a superstar in this business.

Understand, this book is no magic wand. This is meant to be a basic guide to get you up and running the right way or to give you a jump start if you're having trouble along the way. Reading it does not guarantee that you will be opening up the next MTV Music Awards with Britney, Madonna and Christina. But it will teach you what you need to know to break in, polish your craft and hang in there for the long haul. In other words, get it crackin'.

You often hear me say on *Idol* and elsewhere, "What's

up, Dawg?" Sometimes it means, "Hey. How are you?" Other times it means, "What were you thinking?" or "Yo, what's wrong with you. You should know better. Why are you acting like that?" It can also mean, "Wow, you got game."

You have to live in reality, as I like to say. If I'm being honest with you, you have to be honest with yourself. As you read this book and as you make your way through your career, you may want to ask yourself, "What's up, Dawg?"

We're going to take this little journey to see if you have what it takes to get in the game and move on to the next level. And if you do, I'll be there along the way, cheering you along and coaching you through it. I might be yelling and screaming, but it's going to be hot.

So let's see, Dawg, if you've got "What's up?"

Do You Have "It"?

chapter one

IN 1989, I WAS WORKING IN SAN FRANCISCO with Narada Michael Walden, one of the hottest producers in the country at the time. We were making some of the dopest hits of the day, including Whitney Houston's "How Will I Know" and "I Wanna Dance with Somebody," Aretha Franklin's "Freeway of Love" and George Michael and Aretha's duet, "I Knew You Were Waiting."

Demos from unknown artists poured nonstop into the office. We would sit and listen to everything. We heard lots of good songs and hot voices—and, dude, some that were beyond terrible. It wasn't often that a Whitney or an Aretha would come calling.

I'll never forget the day when an unforgettable demo from a young, unknown singer came into the office. A big-name record exec had just signed her and was looking for producers to work on her first album. We played the cassette and couldn't believe what we were hearing.

The singer had written the lyrics and melodies herself. The music had a jazzy, Anita Baker–meets-pop/ R&B sound to it. Beautiful. But it was the singer's voice that took my breath away. Her unbelievably sweet, buttery tones. Her incredible seven-octave range. Her amazing phrasing. And she sang with such conviction and passion.

She had the complete package. I just could not believe how talented this singer was. She had the kind of voice that commands you to listen to the end of a song because you just can't turn it off. The kind of voice you hear on the radio that makes you pull the car over and call the radio station to find out, *yo, who the hell is this?* You want to rush out and buy that song. That music touched you. Affected you. Gave you the chills.

There was no doubt in my mind. She was going to be a star. I knew the public would not deny that voice. This is what we, in the business, look for. She had "it."

The singer? Mariah Carey.

What is "it"?

SO YO, YOU WANT TO KNOW WHAT "IT" is and, more important, if you've got it. The "it" I'm talking about is that rare combination of personality, charisma and talent that can catapult you to stardom.

Michael Jackson, Elvis, Madonna, Mariah Carey, Whitney Houston, Celine Dion, the Beatles, Justin Timberlake, Alicia Keys, Norah Jones, 50 Cent, Britney Spears, Janet Jackson, Snoop Dog, Gwen Stefani, Jay-Z, Beyoncé Knowles and Elton John, among others, all have "it."

The people who have "it" also have that *je ne sais quoi*—that special something that attracts people to them and makes fans want to walk, talk, act and be like them. Look at Michael Jackson. He was a star as a child but exploded onto the scene with *Thriller* in the eighties. How do we know that he had "it"? Everyone was dancing like him. Everyone was dressing like him. Everyone was infatuated with him. He influenced millions of people. Michael Jackson *owned* the eighties.

Same thing with Madonna. She came out in her bra and panties, shocked everyone and dominated the scene. At the height of her popularity, young girls everywhere were trying to emulate her because she was so bold, so uninhibited—and so unique, like nothing you'd ever seen or heard before. She made you ask, *"Whoa, who the hell was that?"*

The Beatles definitely had "it." They pulverized the industry. They rocked the entire world. And today, there are bands still out there trying to emulate what they did. Bands like Coldplay and the Goo Goo Dolls.

Elvis is the king of "it." People did their hair like him. Dressed like him. Talked like him. Even though he's been gone for more than 25 years, they *still* adore him.

These people ruled the planet. They were bigger than the presidents of countries. They represent the pinnacle of "itness."

We ended up producing "I Don't Wanna Cry" on Mariah's first album, *Mariah Carey*, which has hits that are now world famous, including "Vision of Love." The album went multi-platinum. "I Don't Wanna Cry" became a hit song. Mariah shot to stardom, as we knew she would. When we heard her demo that day, we knew that everyone would want to be a part of what she was doing musically.

Her talent has taken her to the top. To me, Mariah, Whitney and Celine are the big three. The best. I refer to them so much on *American Idol* and elsewhere because I've had the pleasure of working with these superstars, who are among the biggest selling artists of all time.

They have each sold more than 100 million albums, an achievement that tops other huge stars who have "it," including Christina Aguilera, Britney Spears, All-American Rejects, Limp Bizkit, 50 Cent and Eminem, to name a few.

The "it" comes naturally

BUT YO, YOU HAVE TO REMEMBER THIS. MOST people who have "it" are born with it. Michael Jackson was born with a God-given gift. When he made his debut in the Jackson Five, he commanded attention. There's no way that an eight-year-old kid from Gary, Indiana, was going to become that famous, that fast, without innate talent.

Prince has a God-given gift. The same with Celine and Elton John. And Elvis—oh my God, what a gift. A true, unbelievable entertainer. He mesmerized a nation with his style, dancing and sound.

Fans loved Elvis because they'd never heard anything like him. He was dope. He had his own form of dance—his own hip-shaking, hip-swiveling movements that people just could not believe. He had a persona. A distinct look, like the old soul singers. I'm sure Chuck Berry had a huge influence on him. And he was dangerous. He sang rock and roll, which at the time people called the devil's music. It was forbidden, which drew people to him all the more.

Like the Beatles, the Grateful Dead, Motown, Michael Jackson and Jimi Hendrix, to name a few, Elvis was able to start a movement. If you want to be a star, you need millions of people following you, like they did. Dude, that's hard to do.

You know the saying "The apple doesn't fall far from the tree." Well, it's true in my family. Zoe, my youngest daughter, loves music with her heart and soul. She's a natural performer and is always putting on shows for the family. I guess she's kind of a ham, like her dad. My son, Jordon, loves playing the drums. But I think he loves skateboarding and break dancing more right now. He is the kid with the 'fro riding a skateboard like Tony Hawk. My oldest daughter, Taylor, also loves music. I remember standing in the kitchen about eleven years ago making hot chocolate for Taylor, who was three at the time. She was sitting in her high chair waiting for me when a Brandy song came on MTV.

When the song ended, she started humming it in the song's exact rhythm and key with an almost perfect pitch.

"Whoa," I thought.

I whipped my head around to look at her.

"Hey, do that again, sweetie," I told her.

She did.

I thought to myself, "She's got it. This kid has something." I'm not just saying this because I'm her dad. I listen to everything with the same critical ear that I use when I listen to demos, songs and *Idol* contestants. Just being able to mimic a song that easily, that exact and correct, is rare at the age of three. That means she has talent.

If you've truly got the gift, singing or playing will come

naturally. Your talent will present itself in perfect form and you'll go, "That was kind of easy." It's like shooting baskets. You may shoot four out of five baskets, no problem. Then five out of five. Easy. But if you stand there and miss five out of five over and over, then it's not natural to you . . . yet.

Being a red carpet regular doesn't guarantee that you have "it"

CELEBRITIES HAVE FANS. THEY HAVE MANAGERS, AGENTS AND publicists. They've recorded albums. They've made it into *People*, *Rolling Stone* or *Vibe*. But just because they've become celebrities doesn't mean they have "it."

Keep in mind that a celebrity is a star by association but isn't someone who necessarily has "it." A lot of the kids who made it into the Top Ten on *Idol* became celebrities—but they didn't go home with the prize. So if you want to be a celebrity, cool. But it means you still don't have "it."

Most of the one-hit wonders out there probably don't have "it." If you're a one-hit wonder, then a hit song created your success—not you. The song was the "it." And if you look on the list of "it" requirements, a great song is conspicuously absent.

So yo, you're asking me: Why wouldn't the song be on the list? A successful song is something that's very nebulous —something you can't always put your finger on. Sometimes a song can rattle the charts, like Justin Timberlake's "Rock Your Body." Beyoncé's "Crazy in Love" featuring Jay-Z. Christina Aguilera's "Beautiful." 50 Cent's "In Da Club." Or classics like Michael Jackson's "Beat It." Elvis' "Love Me Tender." The Beatles' "Ticket to Ride."

A great song is a great song is a great song. You can have a hit, but that's no guarantee that you'll have a long career. You can get maybe two or three of your 15 minutes of fame from it. And remember this. It's very hard to have a hit song. If it were that easy, the music industry wouldn't be in trouble right now.

When I was working as a record exec, I can't tell you how many times I heard another exec say, "Randy. Let's go get some hits." Like you could just go to McDonald's and order some hits. You just can't order up hits to go. All the top songwriters try for that unforgettable song. Sometimes they hit and sometimes they miss. So Dawg, if you think you're going to ride your way into fame on a great song, you have to know, that's no easy road, either.

You want to give 'em chills

KNOWING WHO HAS "IT" IS EXACTLY WHAT I do in the music business and as a judge on *American Idol*. We say to everyone who comes into the *Idol* auditions—"What's going to make us like you over someone else? What's so special about you that we're going to go, 'Wow. We *really* like that'?" I can tell if a person's got "it" as soon as I meet them. I can tell if they have that special charisma. That infectiousness. When I hear singers auditioning for *Idol*, I can tell if they have it vocally as soon as they open their mouths. I can tell by the tone of their voice, their range, their control. You can see how much work they've done or if they are the rarest of the rare and have a God-given gift. And you can see how much work they need to do.

I knew that *Idol*'s first winner, Kelly Clarkson, had it as soon as I heard her sing. Paula, Simon and I often argue about this, but I remember it like it was yesterday. We were in Dallas during the show's first season. It was the end of the afternoon, about 5 or 5:30. We were all tired. We'd heard about 85 kids at that point. We had seen some goofballs and crazy, wild kids, singing all kinds of songs you don't often hear at auditions, like "Silent Night." Just some weirdo people. We had heard some people who were good. But we also heard some people who were terrible.

Then Kelly walked in. Didn't have a particular look. Seemed to me the girl-next-door type. Then whoa! She started her audition and woke us up. I remember thinking, "Oh my God. This girl can *really* sing." The sound of her voice gave me the chills. Kelly was born with a natural gift. I think you can make a lot of headway if you have some talent, but remember those who make it big are usually born with it.

I thought, "If her talent could be shaped and could grow, she could go all the way." I loved her voice. Being a musician, what's always going to excite me first is the voice. I'm looking to get the chills or to be moved in some way. It's not about all the riffs and the runs that people associate with gospel music and try to mimic. It's not about the mechanics. It's about the sound of the voice. If I get the chills from the sound of the voice, that's what does it for me. And I know other people will probably get the chills from it, too. I look for that every time.

Remember—People will equate the sound of your voice with your identity. That sound is your brand. Think about it, when you turn on the radio and hear someone singing, you know immediately—"Oh, that's Madonna. That's Mariah. That's Justin Timberlake. That's R. Kelly." That's their identity on the radio right there. It's like no one else's.

Believing in yourself

ONE OTHER THING THAT STOOD OUT ABOUT KELLY that day in Dallas was her personality. We had a running joke going when she auditioned. We swapped seats. I went and stood on the circle and sang the R. Kelly song "I Believe I Can Fly." She sat in my chair and pretended to be me.

She joked with me. She was funny. She had a cute, engaging personality. And she was so calm and relaxed. Most of all, she sang with conviction. Assurance. She was like, "Let me do my thing because I know I have it." When someone sings with conviction, I don't care when, where or what, you can feel the passion that "I am gonna do this."

Other Idolers who had "it"

IN *IDOL'S* FIRST SEASON, IT WAS CLEAR THAT Kelly had it. We certainly had a healthy Top Ten that year, but there was one other person on the show that season who I think had *straight outta da* Dawg's Mouth—*tip 2*

Think about it. You never see the stars sweat. And if they are a little nervous, you'll never know it because they are prepared beyond belief. The ones who have "it" are never fidgeting onstage or forgetting their lyrics. They have it together.

If you've been rehearsing like crazy, practicing the same song over and over and getting yourself together, you may have slight jitters when you go on an audition or walk onstage, but because you are so beyond ready and so prepared, you'll forget any nervousness and give your best performance. It should be almost effortless at that point.

If you want to cut down on any audition or performance anxiety and be mentally prepared, you have to rehearse nonstop. Singing or playing should become second nature to you—like brushing your teeth. If you're nervous about performing, then get out there and perform. Work out every kink so you can feel more prepared than ever. This will calm you down. And remember this: If your nerves are getting in the way of your performance, nobody's going to see your "itness." So practice as much as you can, Dawg.

"it"—Tamyra Gray, who came in fourth. I thought she should have come in second.

I was hoping to see a standoff between Kelly and Tamyra, just like the standoff we had in the second season between Ruben Studdard, who won, and Clay Aiken, the runner-up. I thought Kelly and Tamyra were the two best singers and performers on the first *Idol*.

Tamyra had the look. The sound. The charisma. She had everything to me. She had "it." She is a great example of someone who has what it takes to make it in the business.

On the night Tamyra lost, she had a terrible cold and couldn't perform up to the level she had throughout the competition. She knew she wasn't at her best. I think it bothered her and that led her to give a performance that wasn't as good as the others she had given.

At that point in the contest, when the competition is so fierce, voters are looking for someone to make a mistake or give a bad performance. Many people who watch shows like this might think, "Oh, this person messed up. This person must not be that good."

Even though Tamyra didn't perform as well as she usually did and was eliminated, she still finished very high—in the Top 5. Of the hundreds of people who audition on *Idol*, very few get record deals. She did. So to me, she is one of the ones who has "it."

Searching for the "it" in you

OK. NOW THAT YOU'RE CLEAR ON WHAT "IT" is and what stars have it and why, let's talk about how you can tell if you have it and how to maximize whatever "itness" you may have. The "it" is the star in you. What you're best at. Why people are drawn to you. This could be your voice, your personality or your dancing ability.

You may already have "it." Well, good for you. But if you don't have the whole package, then I'll help you make the most of whatever "itness" you have.

To figure out what the "it" is in you, you've got to play

up your strengths. But you have to know what your strengths are. If you don't, find an expert who can help you pinpoint your itness.

To find your strengths, you can ask yourself, "What do I do best? What do I sing best? What do I play best? Does it come easily to me? When I take lessons, do I sing and play amazingly well? Do I pick up things easily, like my daughter, who was able to hum the Brandy song back to me in the exact rhythm and key?"

It's rare to be born with true itness, like Elvis or Michael Jackson. But if you have some talent, you can work hard and develop it and possibly get somewhere with it. Many stars that you know and love have done that.

You need someone to tell it to you straight. To tell you if you have "it" or some part of it. Not your family. Not your friends. But a professional. A teacher. A musician. A singer. Somebody in the know who won't lie to you because they don't want to hurt your feelings.

If you don't know anybody like this, then you have to go find them. Ask around. Ask your teachers at school who they would recommend. Ask a friend of the family. Make a few calls. Take the initiative. Take charge of your life.

When you meet with this teacher, musician, singer, etc., ask him or her what you need to work on. What you should do to improve. This may mean taking lessons. Studying music. Practicing. If you have the desire bad enough, you'll do it, Dawg.

This person may say, "Your voice is hot. Your voice is the best thing about you. It needs work, but it's good." So that's what you should be focusing on first. Let the voice be your guide. Work on your voice and try to improve everything else as much as you can.

Ruben and Clay let their voices guide them. The two of them are not runway models. Ruben is no Denzel. And Clay is no Brad Pitt, but it didn't matter. Look how far their talent has taken them. They now have huge careers ahead of them.

So maybe you're not some Tommy Hilfiger model. Maybe you don't look like Britney Spears. Seek out other opportunities for your talent and let your talent be your guide.

You may say, "I'm an OK singer but I'm an incredible dancer and I'm drop-dead gorgeous." Guess what? Look at all the former dancers who have made it big—Madonna. Paula Abdul. Jennifer Lopez. Seek out dancing as your guide and make the kind of music that allows you to show off your dancing prowess.

Forget the autograph

YOU MAY BE LUCKY ENOUGH TO RUN INTO someone famous —a producer, a star, a record exec, an *American Idol* judge, etc. Let them be your pro for the moment. But make sure to ask them *constructive* questions. At this stage, instead of walking up to them and saying, "Hey, sign me" or "Can I have your autograph?" or even "Listen to my demo"—'cause you ain't ready yet to hand out any demos—ask them, "Yo, can I sing for you?" "Is my voice any good? If you were me, what would you do? What part of me would you focus on and sell?"

These are the kinds of questions that will help you get

to the next level. So if you ever bump into Mariah, tell her you're a budding singer and ask her, "What turned the key for you?"

Or if you see Brian McKnight, say, "Yo. What helped you most in your career?" Or you can ask Jonathan Davis from Korn, "What did you do that did the trick for you?"

You need more than "it" to make it

SO YO. SO YOU THINK THAT YOU HAVE a dope voice, a sexy look or a hot personality. You think you just may have what it takes to race up the charts and make it big. Hold on there. You're not done yet. There are a few other things that you need to know.

To reach the top, you need to make sure that your psychological toolbox is well-equipped. You have to first ask yourself: Are you tough enough to stay in the game?

If you're faint of heart and don't take criticism well, you're not gonna make it. Everyone will diss you before they love you. The public. Record executives. A&R reps. Producers. Friends. Family. The competition. Remember the phrase—only the strong survive.

People may diss you for all sorts of reasons. Jealousy. Ego. Their own insecurities. Or because they're just plain mean.

You may hear things like, "Her hair is ugly. I hate his shoes. Her eyes are crooked. He can't sing. She thinks that's talent? She's too fat. He's too skinny. He's so geeky. Look at his nose." In this business, you may hear every negative comment known to man before you hear some positives.

Learning to take constructive criticism well is an important part of your journey. You definitely don't know it all yet. Learn to listen intently to people you trust, take their advice and work on it. You want to know what people think of your performance. After all, this is a people business and you're trying to get better, aren't you?

Later on in the book, I'll talk to you about how having confidence and conviction can help you learn to deal with rejection and criticism, constructive or otherwise. But for now, I'll tell you that you have to get used to rejection. It's going to come at you from all directions. It's just part of the business. When you begin this journey, one of the tools you must have is a belief in yourself. You must have the eye of the tiger. That feeling that nothing is going to stop you if you truly have "it" or some part of "it." The will to go on if somebody says they don't like you. You always hear people say, "How bad do you want it?" Those are the people who get it. And that could be you, if you've got "it" and you're willing to work hard for it.

straight outta da Dawg's Mouth—*tip 3*

Keep in mind that *everybody* hears the disses. Celine heard them. Whitney heard them. Even Mariah. The biggest stars still hear negative things about themselves. But they keep going. They tune it out. And you need to do the same. Tune it out and keep going. Part of keeping it real means developing that tough skin. That's got to be foremost in your mind at all times.

Remember, sticks and stones, man . . .

Can you hear the truth?

ON *IDOL*, SOME PEOPLE SAY SIMON IS THE more truthful judge and Paula and I are so nice. I take offense at this. This means people aren't listening at all to what Paula and I say to the contestants.

You tell me which line is true:

A. "Yo Dawg, that was not good," which is what you've heard me tell contestants, or

B. "That was appalling," which you've heard Simon say.

Guess what, people? We are both saying the same thing. I guess it depends on how you want to hear your information—from the drill sergeant or from your Dawg.

On *Idol*, we have to give it to people straight. We're trying to find the best undiscovered talent in America. I've told people on the show that singing isn't what they should be doing with their lives. I've also told people they could have a career, but that they would have to work extremely hard to make it. I've also told people they're not ready for this level yet.

Believe it or not, man, I know where you're coming from in this department. I've sent demos around as a musician. I've auditioned. I'll be honest here. I don't care what people think about me or say about me because I'm harder on myself than anybody. And I'm a realist. See, that's the thing. You have to keep it real. Some of the things people will say, you'll agree with. Some things you won't.

Even so, people can say stupid things. It happens on *Idol* all the time. People who are auditioning will say to me, "God, you're fat!"

No kidding. As if I don't know that.

On one show, a kid who was pretty angry said, "I hate those judges. Randy is fat. Paula is just plain. And Simon's an a—hole."

Please.

We've already been there. Our skins are so thick it's impossible to hurt us. You think I don't have mirrors in my house? I know what I look like. I keep it real with myself, as I'm telling you to do. We're not the ones up there auditioning. So guess what? The joke's on you.

When someone lashes out like this, I can tell that that person is in trouble psychologically. They can't take constructive criticism. Somebody telling them the truth.

In the 1992 movie *A Few Good Men*, Jack Nicholson's character says, "You can't handle the truth!" It's true. Most people can't, obviously. But you don't want to be in that bunch. You want to hear the truth, accept it, understand it and correct the things that are wrong with you. You'll notice that older people always say, "If I knew then what I know now . . . " That's why you need other people's objectivity about what you are doing. It's what's going to help you go to the top.

But you have to keep the criticism that's coming your way in perspective. Here is where logic comes in. Logic needs to be a number-one part of your psyche. Your outlook should be 75 percent logical and 25 percent emotional. That's not always easy to do. But you have to look objectively at what these people are saying. You want to develop your own talent before you let people drive you with words.

This doesn't mean ignoring reality. If your teacher tells you to work on your vibrato—then work on your vibrato. But if someone is just talking to talk—dodge their negative vibes and just move on. Know who to pay attention to. Know the difference between when people are being vindictive and when they're actually being helpful and truthful.

Experience will help you to figure out the difference between valuable advice and useless disses. But don't worry. This will come with time as you make your way through the business.

Don't be delusional

KEEP IN MIND THAT THERE'S A DIFFERENCE BETWEEN having self-esteem and being delusional. You hear us say the word on *Idol* all the time. When you're delusional, you think you're way, way, way better than you actually are. It means you have marginal talent but think you are the next Tupac, a true leader. The delusional ones—and you know who you are—think they've arrived when they haven't. If you're delusional, you're kidding yourself.

Know how good you are. Know your strengths and weaknesses. It's good to believe in yourself. That's what's going to help you go far in this business. But don't believe you are better than you know you are. Remember to always keep it real with yourself.

Make sure you're in this for the right reasons

EXACTLY WHY ARE YOU TRYING TO BREAK INTO the music biz? For the big house? To pick up chicks? To snag a rich husband? To become a millionaire? Are you keeping real for your game? If not, this is never going to happen for you.

People who are hungry, who really, really want this—and you gotta really, really want this, because it's too much hard work otherwise—will stay in the game. Without the burning desire to make it, you'll fizzle out.

You need a love of music

PEOPLE OFTEN SAY THAT WHAT YOU LOVE IS what you are probably going to be good at or what you're most likely going to do with your life. If you really want to make it in this business, you have to marry music at an early age. You have to give your life to this. You have to do everything you can to try to better yourself and make it. If you don't love music this much, then you are not going to win at this game.

As a kid, I loved music and fell more in love with it the more I played it. My main priority—what was most important to me—was how to get better and how to continue my enjoyment of it. As a result, music has been the center of everything that has happened to me in my life and everything I've done, career-wise. Being a judge on *Idol*, for instance, came out of being a music professional. Every lucky break I've gotten has come through music. So really, music *should* be one of my first priorities.

Even though I'm telling you to focus on your music and improve your craft, you also have to remember to try to keep it all in perspective. It's all about balance. You're not going to be able to love music and your budding career 100 percent of the time. You can't neglect your family, your friends, your education or your job, if you have one. Don't get stupid about this journey. But stay focused.

And remember, while loving music with all your heart is a great start, it's just the beginning.

Hanging in for the long haul

DAWG, ONE OF THE MOST IMPORTANT THINGS YOU need to have in this business is perseverance. We're not sprinting here. This is a marathon. Do you have the perseverance to stay in the real game, no matter what? No matter who says what? No matter what goes on?

It's not going to be easy. It means rehearsing as much as you can, two to four hours a day or more. Taking every gig, everywhere, so you can experience what it's like to sing in front of people, to get over your stage fright and to try new ideas on the job.

It's like putting yourself in a massive boot camp for life and thinking, "I can always improve. I can take constructive criticism well and use it." It means asking for help along the way from professionals who know what they're doing. If somebody says you sing out of tune—and that person has the qualifications to know what "out of tune" means—then listen to them. Your family and friends might have no idea what that means. They might not understand the mechanics.

I worked hard and persevered to get where I am today. Life is good. I'm not alone. Any successful entertainer out there has persevered. You don't get to be Beyoncé, Justin or Alicia and other big stars by not putting in the work. It took all of them a long time to get to where they are. Rehearsing for four hours or more a day. Maybe dancing for five hours or more a day.

On many artists' albums, they record their vocals on and off for months before they are done with the album vocally. Do you have the will to sing the same song in a studio for 10 hours a day? This is the kind of tenacity you'll need to succeed in one of the most competitive businesses around. You need to work as hard as you can. As I said before, it ain't gonna be easy. But it can be done.

As Thomas Jefferson said, "I'm a great believer in luck and I find the harder I work, the luckier I get."

Keep reviewing

AS YOU MAKE YOUR WAY THROUGH THIS BOOK, if you lose your way at any point, go back to the previous chapters and read them over and over again until it all sinks in. Step back and try things from a new angle. Don't give up. Just remember, these words of wisdom will not change. Each time you read them, you'll have a different level of understanding. So let's go, Dawg!

Being Dawgmatic About Getting Your Skills Together

chapter two

THE SUGGESTIONS I'M MAKING TO YOU IN THIS book are some of the things I did to make it in the music business. My late father, Herman C. Jackson Sr., was an Exxon plant foreman. My mother, Julia Jackson, was a homemaker. My family didn't have any connections in the business, so I made my own, starting when I was just a kid. I played everywhere possible, got to know as many people in the industry as I could and soaked up everything—things you should be doing as you get your music career going. Remember, you are a sponge right now.

In the next few pages, I'm going to tell you how I went from jamming on my mother's front porch as a kid to playing with greats like Mariah Carey and *NSYNC. Some of the lessons I learned when I was coming up may help you as you make your way in the business.

If you know me, you know that music is in my blood. It always has been and always will be. Growing up in Baton

Rouge, Louisiana, music was everywhere, dude. In the 'hood where I lived. In clubs around town. In school. And definitely in church.

My brother, Herman Jr., and my sister, Sue Ann, always had some kind of music playing around the house. James Brown. Motown. The Supremes. And I lived in the South, so church music was a big part of my life. On Sundays, I heard people sing with passion, soul and heart—not for money, but for God. That stuck with me.

My love for music began early. I started messing around with the saxophone, the guitar and the drums in grade school, experimenting with music. My brother had a band that would practice in my parents' garage. Man, I loved listening to them. They moved and motivated me.

Another big influence in my life at the time was a bass player named Sammy Thornton. He and his band, Big Bo Melvin and the Nitehawks, used to rehearse on Sammy's front porch around the corner from my house. They were unbelievable. The whole neighborhood would stand shoulder to shoulder, dancing and singing along as they played R&B and Top Forty hits into the night.

Yo man, I was blown away by their passion and how they made the whole crowd feel so good. I thought, "That's me. I want to be a part of this." I knew that I wanted to make music because their songs made my soul come alive. I knew I wanted to make music my life.

Starting one of the best chapters of my life

ONE OF THE MOST IMPORTANT THINGS I CAN recommend is to find a great teacher or mentor to help you. After hearing

Sammy on his front porch, I asked him if he would teach me the bass. I thought he was a genius. He became my mentor, 'cause yo, my man could play the hell out of the bass. So dude, ask somebody you look up to or admire to teach you or to lead you to someone who can.

When I was learning how to play the bass, I felt like a kid in a candy store. I wanted to practice every day. Sammy taught me how to play all the Stevie Wonder songs from "I Was Made to Love Her" to "Signed, Sealed, Delivered" —songs where the bass was so dynamic and the music was so rich.

I started my own band and played on my mom's front porch, trying to do what Sammy did. Trying to do what my brother and all these other people did. I was only in seventh grade, but we played shows all over town. We'd go out, get gigs and play for free. We would just practice every day, all day long. Anytime we heard someone was playing on a local college campus or in a park, we were there. We lived in the music store, soaking up conversations, listening to the radio, just going crazy with music.

Keeping it moving and moving

WHEN I GOT TO ROBERT E. LEE HIGH SCHOOL in Baton Rouge, I played varsity football and threw shot put and discus on the track and field team. I loved sports and was a great athlete, but music was still in the forefront for me. I joined the high school marching band, the high school symphony and the high school jazz band. I was playing in the local youth symphony. I played acoustic upright bass in the orchestra for local theater shows like Porgy and Bess. I was playing the saxophone. I started playing piano. I got turned on to rock and started listening to people like Jimi Hendrix, AC/DC, Led Zeppelin and Deep Purple. I threw myself full throttle into music, loving the joy that it brought to my soul.

I knew that I had a gift and wanted to learn everything I could about music. So once again, I sought help from people in the know, just like I'm telling you to do. This time it was the high school band director, John Gerbrecht, who took me under his wing and taught me about music.

He had a band that would play "casuals"—weddings, parties or bar mitzvahs—whatever was going on around town. Everyone in the band was about 40 years old, so you can imagine my surprise at being asked to play with them at 16.

After that, I just started playing whatever gigs I could. One job led to another, which helped me grow by leaps and bounds. Keep in mind, Dawg, that I was working mostly with people older and more experienced than me. I became the biggest sponge on the planet. I listened to what they said, how they talked and how they played music. I would even ask these older cats which songs they liked on the radio and why, to get their perspective. To know how to do something well, you have to understand it from all angles.

Learning from the best

IN MY JUNIOR YEAR, I WON A GRANT from the National Association of Jazz Educators and the National Endowment for the Arts that gave me the opportunity to study with anyone I wanted. I picked Chuck Rainey, a bass player who was on Ben Vereen's TV show at the time. He had played on records with the likes of Steely Dan, Michael Jackson, Ray Charles and Aretha Franklin. He's one of the guys who helped put the electric bass on the map. He was a true master.

So, at the end of my junior year, I flew to Los Angeles, where I immersed myself in his world. For a kid from Baton Rouge, it was just unbelievable. I went with him to the music studio, where he recorded a session with Donald Byrd and the Blackbyrds. I went with him to the TV studio, where he taped Ben Vereen's show. I took lessons from him and learned everything I could from him. I asked him which instruments I should play and why. Which brand of bass he recommended. It was on-the-job training. And I wasn't even out of high school yet.

straight outta da Dawg's Mouth—*tip 4*

At a young age, dude, I started taking on everything at once, like I still do today. I went from being a workaholic kid to the workaholic adult I am now. As far back as I can remember, I was always busy as hell.

Sometimes I think I'm crazy. But you know, you have to be a bit over-the-top to chase your dreams this hard. It consumes you, but in a positive way. Everyone I know who is beyond successful works as hard if not harder than I do and as hard if not harder than before they made it. This profession you are choosing is about putting in the work. So if you don't have the stomach for this, you're going to have to choose something else.

Getting my studio chops

IT WAS DURING THIS TIME THAT I FIRST began doing session work—playing background music on an album. Individual artists usually don't have their own bands, so they hire session musicians to play for them. Ever wonder who does all those records for Madonna, Christina or Celine and others? Session musicians who come in and play for them.

I learned about studio etiquette, how to mike my amp and how to play with headphones on. I needed to know all of this so I would know what I was doing later on. I played bass on an album with blues singer Irma Thomas and then with a local band called John Fred and the Playboys, who'd had a national hit with the 1968 song "Judy in Disguise."

My first big break

WHEN IT CAME TIME FOR COLLEGE, I GOT a football scholarship but chose the music route over sports. I followed my brother to Southern University in Baton Rouge to study with Alvin Batiste, who was the premiere jazz studies teacher in my area and one of the best in the country.

During the summer between sophomore and junior years, I did nothing but practice because I knew there were things I needed to work on. I was keeping it real with myself. I put myself through boot camp. I skipped parties. I played day and night. My hard work paid off, yo. In my senior year, I got my first big break when I auditioned for jazz rock fusion great Billy Cobham. I mean, in the jazz rock fusion world, he was the man. A drummer extraordinaire who had played with greats like Miles Davis. A true pioneer.

Auditioning against 30 other bass players, I got the gig —a chance to join his band, make albums with him for Columbia Records in New York City and go on tour with him. This was my entrance into the big time. We played everywhere and I got to know a lot of influential people who would help me throughout my career.

I didn't know it at the time, but so many people I met in my younger years would later become part of my life in some way. While I was playing with Billy Cobham, for example, I met Narada Michael Walden, a producer I would later work with in San Francisco, who became an integral part of my success. If you are out there playing gigs, meeting people and networking, it will happen for you, too.

San Francisco bound

AFTER MORE THAN A YEAR OF TOURING WITH Billy Cobham and making two albums with him, I went back and finished college. I taught music for a summer in Texas and then went on to San Francisco, where I joined Narada Michael Walden's production team as a musician, songwriter and staff producer.

I played bass and co-wrote songs on probably 50 or 60 albums with Narada Michael Walden. I worked with superstars including Whitney Houston, Mariah Carey, Lionel

Ritchie and Aretha Franklin, to name a few. My career as a session player took off. I worked with Blue Oyster Cult, Michael Bolton, Clarence Clemons, Joe Cocker, Celine Dion, Hall and Oates, Herbie Hancock, Sister Sledge and Billy Idol—the Britneys, Justins and Goo Goo Dolls of their time.

A lot of doors started opening for me. Wanting to play as much as possible, Santana's Tom Coster, Journey drummer Steve Smith, Journey guitarist Neil Schon and I started a jazz fusion band in San Francisco and had a great time doing it. Along the way, those guys introduced me to the rest of the members of Journey. I met them in the studio when they were recording "Any Way You Want It," a song now used in a famous Ford commercial. When I met them, I never thought that I would someday join their band. At the time, I was just networking and meeting people, just like I'm telling you to do. You never know where a good hook-up with somebody will lead.

Networking, hanging out and meeting people also led me to play in a pick-up band with the Grateful Dead's Bob Weir and Jerry Garcia, jazz fusion great Tony Williams, Carlos Santana and Weather Report's Wayne Shorter, among others.

My rock dreams become reality

IN 1983, STEVE SMITH, NEIL SCHON AND JOURNEY'S lead singer, Steve Perry, hooked me up as a session musician with the group, ghost playing on their album *Frontiers*. It was such a great band. Steve Perry is one of the all-time greatest singers, ever.

Journey split up. When they reunited, I became a member of the band. Life as a rock and roll star was unbeliev-able. There is no greater experience than being on stage and having 100,000 people sing the words to your song with you. Crazy. We had tons of fans who would mob the hotels wherever we stayed. They swarmed our cars. Our buses. Imagine a kid from the 'hood living this life. It was the whole rock and roll fantasy dream, dude. Limos. Private planes. Cash flowing. The best of everything. It was the American dream. Just like on *Idol*.

The sessions years

AFTER LIVING IN SAN FRANCISCO FOR 10 YEARS, I moved to LA, where I was playing a lot of sessions with some of the biggest names in the business. I made more than a thou-sand albums with stars such as Bob Dylan, Don Henley, Lionel Ritchie, Bruce Springsteen, Bon Jovi, Elton John, Billy Joel, Sammy Hagar, Kenny G., Richard Marx and the late Robert Palmer.

But after years of playing bass as a session player, I felt that I had hit a wall. I wanted to do something else. I had been developing a career in producing and songwriting. Then a friend of mine, legendary producer and A&R exec David Kahne, gave me a leg up and helped me find a job in A&R at Columbia Records. And that's how I started in the executive pool. I started as a VP and moved up to senior VP of A&R and staff producer at Columbia.

A&R people are responsible for everything associated with making a hit record. They are to me the heart and soul of a record company. They are responsible for finding pro-ducers, songwriters and musicians to work on an album.

They look for hit songs. They find and sign new talent and work with existing artists to make sure they stay on the road to success. I became Mariah's A&R guy and as fate would have it, I became Journey singer Steve Perry's A&R guy when he did a solo record at Columbia. The good things in my life just seem to follow me.

After eight years at Columbia I moved on to MCA as a senior VP of A&R and a staff producer. In 2002, I got the thrill of a lifetime when I won a Grammy Award for co-producing Gladys Knight's album *At Last*.

But for all the fun I was having producing and continuing to play bass on other people's albums here and there, I was getting bored working in corporate America. Being a creative guy in corporate America can be tough. The industry just wasn't creative enough for me anymore. To me, it lost its edge. I'd had a fair bit of success, but the job was just not me. There was something missing.

In a bit of a shocker, there was a big shake-up at the label and I got fired...WOW! But guess what? I was relieved, having wanted to quit for so long. I was elated, to everyone's disbelief. But when you know you got game, you never have to worry or be nervous. One door closes and seven bigger, better ones open.

Never look at closed doors. Just remember to keep looking ahead. There's a saying that if you stay at the dance too long (or in my case, the record company), you will miss out or lose—something. It's like when you're eating Thanksgiving dinner. You eat 'til you feel like you're almost full, then put the fork down and walk away.

straight outta da Dawg's Mouth—*tip 5*

I have this rule that I call "The Dawg's Seven-Year Switch." I believe that every seven years you need to make some kind of change in your career or in your growth or add a new twist. Every seven years I do something that shakes me out of my normal, scheduled life. If you become complacent, you will stay stagnant. You gotta keep growing. When you stop, it's a wrap.

Oh, no—not a reality show

IN 2002, JUST AFTER I LEFT MCA, JEFF FRASCO, a friend from the talent agency Creative Artists Agency, called and told me about *Idol*. At first I was like, "I don't want to do this. TV is corny and cheesy as hell." I wasn't a big fan of TV at the time. But then I stepped back and thought to myself, "Maybe I should check this out." I saw a few episodes of the show's British version, the hugely successful *Pop Idol*. One of its judges was a brutally honest record exec named Simon Cowell. I thought the show was hilarious and just what the American music scene needed at the time—something to shake it up. Being a judge on *American Idol* has been a great ride, but I'm sure a lot of the rejected contestants you've seen don't feel the same way...

Where you should begin

SO DUDE, YOU SAW THE CRAZY PATH I took to get to where I am today. And here you are, just starting out. You think you have a good voice. You've touched base with some professionals you respect who think that you may have "it" or some sort of "it." You've asked a lot of questions and you've done all of your homework so far. So you want to know, where do you go from here?

Finding a teacher

THE FIRST THING YOU WANT TO DO TO lay the groundwork for your success is to find a teacher who will keep it real with you. You want someone who is going to correct the things you're doing wrong and prevent you from developing bad habits that can hurt you down the road. You want someone you can trust to turn you into a much better singer, performer or musician. I'm telling you, Dawg, you don't want to show up at any audition and have someone tell you that you suck, especially if it's on TV. Imagine the ridicule you're going to get when you go home. Baby, how you gonna live that down?

To figure out who the best teacher in your area is, ask people who have the qualifications to know. Don't ask the guy behind the counter at 7-Eleven. Don't ask a kid playing the drums at a pep rally when his band sounded awful. Don't ask your buddy who's standing next to you cooking fries at Burger King. If you don't know what good singing is, listen to your favorite records by your favorite artists and let them guide you.

To find the right teacher, you have to know what your best skill is. If your strong suit is singing, then you have to find the best vocal teacher in town to work with. You go to the best teacher because that person will take you farther than anything else.

The people to ask about finding a teacher? Your music teacher at school. Someone you saw in a band or at a local concert who rocked the house. A music store employee. Your cousin's piano teacher. Your friend's dad who's in the music business.

If you're talking to someone who sings or plays an instrument, ask them, "Did you take lessons? Who taught you? Do you know who is really good in the area? Where can I find them? Can I use your name and say that you sent me?"

Make sure to thoroughly check out the teacher before you sign up for lessons. Talk to some of the teacher's other students. Find out as much as you can about the teacher's background. Where did he study? Where did she perform? How long has he been doing this? Find out if the prices she's charging are in keeping with what others charge. And remember, just because this person is a great performer or musician doesn't mean this person is a great teacher.

When you meet the teacher, ask him or her what you'll be doing each week. Ask about teaching style. What goals he or she might have for you. If it sounds good to you, then sign up. And go with your gut. If something doesn't feel right, move on.

What you should be learning

IF YOU ARE TAKING LESSONS, THEN YOU SHOULD be learning about vibrato—the pulsing of your voice. Is it too fast or too slow? What can you do to strengthen it? You should be working on using the right vocal breathing techniques. Do you take a breath after two words or five words? Your audience can hear the pacing. You should be working on rhythm. Are you singing in time with the beat? Do you have control over your breathing? Can you control your vibrato? What about tone—the sound of your voice? Do you have a pleasant tone or do you always sound sad when you sing? Is it low? Is it high? Is it full enough? Is it too dark or too muzzled? Too cloudy-sounding? Too thin?

Does the sound of your voice make people want to listen to you? What is your range? Can you sing only five notes? How high or how low can you go? You want to make sure you have enough range so that you can sing bigger melodies.

You should focus on sight reading. You should learn what pitch is. Are you on pitch or are you singing out of tune all the time? Can you even hear the pitch? If you can't hear the pitch, you have no business singing.

But one of the most important things for a singer is ear training, ear training and more ear training. This is what music, other people's voices or your voice sound like to your ear. If you can't hear that note, you're not going to be able to sing that note. You need to hear it in your head before you sing it. You have to be able to hear what great tone is and you have to be able to hear what tone you are making. You have to be able to hear if you or other people are

It's important for you to learn from somebody who is totally outside of the box, who has all the objectivity in the world, hopefully, to teach you what you need to know and to help you improve. You need a Randy, Paula or Simon keeping it real in your life at all times. If we're not there, just imagine our voices and what we would tell you. On *Idol*, you may hear us say a lot, "You suck. Quit or get better." That's your goal when you're working with a teacher. You want feedback. That is the only way to improve.

Your teacher should be someone who will enhance your skills. Sometimes in the *Idol* auditions you see people come in with a pitch pipe their teacher has given them to help them find the starting note. And they still can't sing. That student may have hired that teacher based on somebody's recommendation, without checking the teacher out. Remember—you have to do your homework if you want to get your groove on.

Some people think they don't need a vocal teacher. They listen to the radio and sing "Crazy in Love" by Beyoncé and they say, "I sound just like her already. I don't need lessons." Wrong. Singing incorrectly can damage your vocal cords and sometimes can cause permanent damage. If you're not singing correctly, then you won't have the power you need. It's why you're hoarse. The smart people who are in this for real will get up off it and get the best voice teacher they can. So take care of business, man, and go do the same.

singing in tune or not. You have to learn to train your ear to hear things exactly and correctly.

You may think you're not tone deaf when you really are. Being tone deaf is the inability to hear pitches or tones correctly as they relate to melody. You've heard me ask people on *Idol*, "Are you tone deaf?" Of course, they don't think they are. You have to live in reality. If you are tone deaf, singing or playing may not be for you.

So you wanna join a band? Not so fast . . .

SO WHILE YOU'RE LOOKING FOR RECOMMENDATIONS FOR A teacher, you may be meeting singers and band members in your area. You hit it off with a young drummer who gave you a great lead on someone who might be able to teach you. That got you thinking, "Hey, why don't I ask this guy if I can jam with him and his band?"

Stop right there! Don't even think about asking to join a band right now. You're not even remotely ready. Most people at this stage say, "Hey. Why don't we get together and jam or something?" At this stage, you don't even know what you're doing, even though you might think you do.

You can jam—but by yourself at this point. You need to practice as much as you can to get yourself ready for the next level. Dude, you'll be playing with other people—just later on. Just focus on the basics for now. Put it this way. It's like saying, "I'm going to join the varsity basketball team at school, but I don't know how to play hoops yet. I can learn when I get there." No you can't. You need to know what you're doing first before you can join a band.

What about the cheddar—the cha-ching?

LESSONS COST MONEY. THEY DON'T COME CHEAP. IF you don't have extra cash lying around for lessons, figure out how you can pay for them. Maybe you can ask your parents or a family member to help out. See if you can get a weekend job so you can save up enough money to pay for them—even if you can only afford one or two lessons a month. No matter how many lessons you take, they're only going to help you get better.

straight outta da Dawg's Mouth—*tip 7*

You have to be able to know for yourself what's hot and what isn't when it comes to music. You also need to be able to tell if the people giving you advice are truly in-the-know. To do that, you have to learn what is good and what is not. As I said earlier, if you don't understand the difference between good and bad, you need to learn, Dawg.

One way to do this is to listen to as much music as possible and to watch people perform in videos or live on stage. Another great way is to ask people if you can observe them working, like I did with Chuck Rainey in LA. You may not be doing what they're doing for a while. But you can learn so many things while watching a professional do it. You don't need to do this with a big star, just somebody you think is talented in your area.

"Trial and error it" with your teacher

LET'S SAY SIX OR SEVEN MONTHS HAVE GONE by and you don't think you're improving. People may say to you, "Yo, dude. You're taking two lessons a week and you're not getting any better. What's goin' on with you?"

If you're not sure that you've found the right teacher, here's a way to test it. Show up at an audition, open mike night at a club or a contest to gauge where you are. Not to win, but just to see how your development is going.

Some people do this on *Idol* and when they sing, they're horrible. So we'll ask, "Who told you that you could sing?"

"My teacher," they'll say.

Yo, how can this be?? If your teacher says you can sing and you show up for an audition and people tell you that you suck, please lose the teacher! Dump him or her IMMEDIATELY and go on to someone else.

If you don't think you can trust your teacher's abilities—NEXT. If you're saying to yourself, "Now that I've been studying with this person, I don't think he knows what he's doing"—NEXT.

Don't be afraid. This is your future. You have no allegiance to this particular teacher. I meet people all the time who say, "I'm studying with a certain vocal teacher who I love. They've really helped me a lot," and when they sing, I want to run and hide.

There are no allegiances to be formed yet. The only allegiance you have at this point is to yourself. Strive to do everything you can to make it happen for you. You're trying to get it together. And dude, that may mean making some hard decisions. But in the long run, you'll be glad you did.

Ron Anderson is the guru of voice. He is, in my opinion, the best voice teacher in LA and one of the best in the world. He is an international performer and the pro the stars turn to when they need help. His students include Gwen Stefani, Nelly Furtado, Mary J. Blige, Natalie Imbruglia, Enrique Iglesias, Jonathan Davis of Korn, TLC, Stone Temple Pilots, Chris Cornell of Soundgarden and Audioslave, Bjork, LeAnn Rimes, Eddie Vedder of Pearl Jam, Kelly Clarkson, Justin Guarini and Tamyra Gray, among many others.

RANDY: So Ron, how do you recommend finding a teacher?

RON: Finding the right teacher is exceedingly difficult. Finding one through word of mouth is the best way to do it. I would stay away from people who advertise.

When someone recommends a teacher to you, make sure to look at the teacher's background. Who have they trained? What do their students sound like? You don't want to sound like anyone else. If everyone sounds alike, stay away.

Before signing up, ask the teacher if you can observe some lessons. Listen to his or her students sing. If you don't like what you hear, go elsewhere. For example, if you hear a break in the student's voice—meaning the voice isn't even from top to bottom—and the teacher can't help the student overcome that, that's a big problem. Walk away.

You should also take a trial lesson. Book an hour and pay for the lesson. Don't just take someone's word for it that this teacher is good. This teacher may work for them, but not for you.

You'll also want to hear the teacher sing. The first time I met with Janet Jackson, she said, "Sing something for me, would you please?" She was so shocked that I could sing that she just about fell over because most teachers, believe it or not, can't. If the teacher can't sing well, how is he or she going to teach you what to do? Whatever faults the teacher has will be passed on to you. We learn by listening.

Once you find the right teacher, never let him or her go. Placido Domingo gave me that very advice. He said that when you find a teacher who knows what he or she is doing, if the teacher moves, you move too. He is absolutely right. That's how difficult it is to find the right teacher for you.

RANDY: How will you know if you've chosen the right teacher?

RON: Your throat will tell you whether this teacher is right or not. If you walk out of a voice session feeling hoarse or vocally tired, then you have gone to the wrong person and you are singing incorrectly. You want a teacher who will show you how to use your voice exactly as it should be used without stressing the voice or putting pressure into the lar-ynx itself.

RANDY: What should you be learning?

RON: You should be learning how the breath works. If the teacher talks about lifting up and pulling in the diaphragm, you are in the wrong place. If the teacher starts talking about the diaphragm as a support mechanism, then you should think about leaving. Thirty-eight years ago, Dr. Frank Cornell at the Juilliard Convention in New York medically proved that it was not the diaphragm that supports the human voice. The intercostal muscles and the rib cage support the human sound. The intercostal muscles are the muscles in between the ribs. The diaphragm is like a faucet. It controls the quality and the quantity of air but does not support the voice.

You should also learn about the motor functions of the breath. The breath is the engine. If the breath is not running properly, nothing will run properly. The most important thing in the beginning is getting the breath correct.

You should also learn about power. It's not like trying to squirt the garden hose a little farther to get to the high note. It's not locking the larynx together to push more air through the voice to get the power. Power comes from resonance and focus. It should never feel like you're using your throat, ever, to get power.

You need to learn how to power your voice correctly. Never let a teacher tell you, "Louder, louder. Scream!" If so, you are definitely in the wrong place. You need to learn how to power your voice. A good example is Aretha Franklin. When she really cranks it up, she is barely singing. She's cruising. You need to learn to do that, also. You should also learn about bridging the voice so it becomes one even sound from top to bottom.

RANDY: How much do lessons cost?

RON: A good teacher with some credibility will charge at least $75 for a half hour. If you go to somebody for $15 an hour, unfortunately it's not the money you're losing, it's the time. You can always make the money up, but not the time. If you don't find somebody who really knows what they're doing, that can hurt you instead of help you.

RANDY: How long should you study?

RON: You should study voice for a minimum of five years. That means at five years, you have really mastered your voice. But you'll never be done. As long as you're singing, there's always something to work on.

RANDY: How do you know if you're improving?

RON: Tape each lesson with the teacher. Use the tapes to learn and practice. After three or four months, go back and listen to the first tape you made. If there's not much of a difference, scram.

Rehearsing is key, Dawg

REHEARSING IS MORE IMPORTANT THAN EVER AT THIS stage because you're setting a course for what's going to be your benchmark—the way you're going to keep yourself fit as a singer or as a musician. Practice, practice and practice some more. Now is not the time for chillin'. You should be rehearsing two to four hours a day. You have to be disciplined about it. You have to set up a rehearsal schedule so that you are practicing every day at the same time. You commit to it. You marry it.

At this point, you should still be practicing by yourself. You are getting yourself ready for what's to come. This is your time, whether you sing along with records, after your warm-up exercises, or do whatever it is that your teacher has instructed you to do. Rehearsing is something you will do for the rest of your life, when you need to practice or when you feel you need to improve in some way. You won't always need to practice for two to four hours a day. But set the pattern now.

Always keep improving

LET'S SAY YOU FIND A GOOD TEACHER. YOU feel like you're getting better. This person is helping you to stretch your skills. You're working on increasing your range. Trying not to sound too nasal. Singing with feeling.

But don't forget that it doesn't hurt to get other people's opinions at this point. If you happen to run into another voice teacher or a professional singer, ask them where they think you stand. You can say, "Would you mind listening to me sing for a minute? Would you please tell me what you like about my voice and what needs work?" Do that as often as you can.

That person may say, "Your vibrato is too fast. Yo, what is this, Alvin and the Chipmunks?" They may say you aren't taking breaths in the right place. Listen and learn.

Don't jump in before you are ready

YOU'VE BEEN TAKING LESSONS FOR EIGHT MONTHS NOW. Your teacher says you need about another six months of lessons, but you think you're ready for the big time. You say, "I'm tired of waiting. I want it to happen now."

I can't tell you how many times I've heard that one. Take a deep breath, step back and think about what you're doing. Take a hard look at where you are. Don't fool yourself into thinking you're ready before it's time.

When you are ready to launch yourself into the big leagues, you want to be beyond ready. This is how I felt after I spent that summer between sophomore and junior years in college playing every day and night, fine-tuning my skills. I felt confident. Ready to take on any musical challenge that came my way.

Don't forget that your competition is tough. People who come to audition for *Idol* hear some of the competition singing their faces off as they wait in line to see us. Singing beautifully. And they start getting a little jittery, going, "Wow, I didn't know people here were that good. This is making me nervous." You have to be prepared.

straight outta da Dawg's Mouth—*tip 8*

Remember, you've gotta keep it real with yourself. You can never let your ego take over. You can't say that you're there yet when you're not. You must always remember three things—humility, compassion and listening. Always be humble. Show compassion to others, and by all means, the most important thing you can do, if you have "it," is to become the world's greatest listener.

The music business is extremely competitive. This is the Olympics, yo. You have to strive to be the best. You need to do everything you can to win. The only way to win this race is to be beyond ready. Remember, the person who shows up at the right time with all the goods—voice, sound, talent and vibe—will get the prize.

Check yourself before you wreck yourself

IN THIS GAME, YOU NEED TO SET SHORT- and long-term goals for yourself. You need goals to gauge where you are in your development and to pinpoint your success level. Without goals, you will fall flat on your face and will wander off your path.

Once you find a good teacher, you need to set your first goal. Let's say the teacher says you need to work on your tone, pronunciation and breathing. So you say, "Between six to eight months from now, I want to master these skills. I'm gonna test myself by going to open mike night or karaoke night at the local club where I'm gonna sing in front of some strangers. I'm gonna turn the place out."

This could be your first test. Yes, the people there may all be partying. No, they probably don't know much about singing, but they'll give you an initial sense of where you stand. That's how you can "check and balance" yourself in the short term. You need touch-ups and tune-ups all the time to prevent yourself from forming bad habits.

When you get off stage that night, you also want to see if there are some professionals there who will keep it real with you. Stay away from asking Joe Public what they think

—because they don't really know what to tell you about what is right or wrong with your performance. All they can tell you is if they liked it. They may like you 'cause you're cute, not because you sing well. On *Idol*, we told somebody, "If we were judging Beauty Queen Idol, you'd win. But we're judging singing. You're very cute, but you can't sing!" You want to grow and find out how to get better.

Make sure to ask the professionals, "How did I do? What was good? What wasn't so great?" You want to find out from them because they're hopefully going to tell you the truth. Then you can see what you need to improve.

To find out who the professionals are in the club or at open mike night or wherever you decide to sing, you have to do your homework first. You have to go to the bar or the club or wherever it is that you're performing, and find out if any musicians or singers hang out there.

Long-term goals

IN THE LONG TERM, YOUR TEACHER CAN HELP you decide when you're ready to try to go for that record deal or to audition for a show like *Idol*. It's up to you and your teacher where you should head in the long term. You may say to the teacher, "In two years, I want to be on *American Idol* or on *Star Search*," or "I want to be in my own band in two years" or "In three years, I want to try and get a record deal." So you give yourself a two- or three-year goal to shoot for.

If the teacher tells you that you won't be ready for change, you might want to consider switching teachers.

This teacher may just want to keep you as a lifetime student to make money off of you. Now you can be a lifetime student, but you still need to set goals, go for your dream and watch out that you're not taken.

If all this sounds hard as hell, it is. But this is your mission, should you choose to accept it. Dawg, you can do it.

Music to a Dawg's Ears

chapter three

A'IGHT, HERE YOU ARE. YOU FOUND
THE RIGHT teacher and you're
practicing as much as possible. But
yo, is your sound on the right track?
To make it in this business, you have
to know who you are musically. Are
you more of a Norah Jones or a Missy
Elliott? A Justin Timberlake or a 50 Cent? An Ashanti
or a Gwen Stefani? A John Mayer or a Snoop Dogg?
Figuring this out could mean the difference between signing with a major label—or going nowhere.

As I was getting my career going, one of the things I
wanted to be was a singer, just like you might. I loved Sly
Stone. I loved James Brown. I wanted to be like these people. I made a demo and shopped it around. I eventually got
my own record deal, but the record never came out and I
never went anywhere as a recording artist. I sang background on a bunch of albums and on stage for Journey. I
have a decent voice, but if I could sound like anyone in the
world, I would want to sound like Stevie Wonder.

But guess what? I never even came within 10 million light years of approaching Stevie Wonder vocally. Still, this is what I wish I could sound like. But remember, what we want is not always what's right for us. In your journey to the top, you have to be ready to accept who you are musically and what's good for you as opposed to what you want. It's that wanting that always gets you in trouble.

Everyone wants to be something they're not. It takes people a long time to come to grips with accepting who they are. In this chapter, you are going to figure out what your musical style is and to learn to accept it. You don't want to play mind games trying to convince yourself that you are the next Mariah Carey when you are really a C-level Mya.

A guy who's fat with brown curly hair and freckles may decide, "I'm gonna be the next Gavin Rossdale or P. Diddy." No, you're not! You have to be realistic. Reality is the best friend that you have. Learn to love reality. Remember, you have to keep it real if you want to get your groove on.

straight outta da Dawg's Mouth—*tip 9*

If you can figure out who you are musically, and become the best at that style, your career could take off. This means always staying true to yourself—not to who you think you are or who you want to be. Learn to love and accept who you are and not who you want to be.

Knowing your musical style can help you in so many ways

FIGURING OUT WHO YOU REALLY ARE MUSICALLY AND what you do best will help you reach your short- and long-term goals. Knowing which stars have the musical style you want will serve as a rough guide for the look, stage presence and vocal sound you'll need for that type of music.

Knowing your style will help you focus your energies so you can sharpen your skills. Let's say your musical style is similar to Avril Lavigne's. Then you'll know what kind of vocal teacher to choose, what kind of songs to sing, what kind of songs to listen to and, down the road, what kind of producer to hire.

If you don't pick a musical niche, you'll become the jack of all trades and styles and the master of none. I see it all the time on *Idol*. We'll ask someone auditioning, "Why are you here?"

And they'll boldly reply, "Because I think I can be the next American Idol." (Between you and me, half the time they don't even know what that means.) So they'll sing something very theatrical, like they belong in an off-, off-, way-off-Broadway musical in New York City.

And we'll say, "You can sing, but your voice is better suited for theater."

"No problem," the wannabe will say. "I can sing something more pop, something more R&B, something jazzier, or something more alternative. What do you want?"

Stop! Stop! Stop! (You know I love to say things three times . . .) It's not what I want. It's what you want. This tells me that you don't know who you are. And you know what?

No one's going to care if you don't know. It's your responsibility to find out who you are first, and that's what you should be selling.

Knowing your musical style can help you in your career down the road. I've seen so many record companies sign artists who have no idea who they are. They may take a year or so to make a record. Market it. Get it out there. And when it's finished? They still haven't made the right record.

I recently heard a girl who just signed with a big label. Someone said, "Her sound is like Al Green meets Aretha." I thought she was more LeAnn Rimes. Big difference there. Remember, you have to know who you are so others will, too.

When I was doing A&R and I met artists who weren't sure who they were musically, I would say to them, "I don't know who you are and you don't know who you are, so guess what? I ain't signing you. I'm not spending my company's money and time trying to figure out who you are. I need to sign stars who know who they are."

Michael Jackson knew who he was when he was a kid. He wasn't singing country. He was singing pop R&B. Elvis knew who he was. He wasn't trying to sing opera songs. Mariah, Whitney, Celine, Aretha, Bob Dylan, Bruce Springsteen and Billy Joel figured out who they were.

So yo, you probably don't know what your musical style is yet—most other people don't, either. That's one of the biggest problems people have when they audition for *Idol*. You may hear me say "Who are you?" when they step before us. You look like Jewel, but you sound like Macy Gray and dance like Britney Spears. You can't be everyone.

Finding your musical style is the most important step right now. 'Cause, once again, if you don't know who you are, what you're best at and what your musical style is, you'll stay in the same place forever. You won't grow. Embrace your strengths. 'Cause honestly, everyone I know who's made it big played up theirs.

Zeroing in on your musical style

TO FIND YOUR MUSICAL STYLE YOU HAVE TO ask yourself, "What type of music am I best at? What kind of singing will give me the best chance in such a competitive market? Would it be best for me to try to be a pop singer or a musician? Am I best at R&B? Does my voice or my instrument lead me there? Am I best at trying to play or sing jazz? Country? Theater or opera? Hip-hop? Alternative music?"

What you're best at and what you love may be two completely different things. "Trial and error it" to find out where your musical strengths lie. Keep an open mind and try out every style you can. You only want to do what you're best at. You don't see Jay-Z making jazz albums.

Listen to songs in each genre. Sing them. See how well you do. Study the artists who have made it big singing in that style. Does this feel right to you? As you try different styles, ask yourself, "Which style do I sing or play best?"

Don't decide alone. Let your teacher and others help you, because you will always veer toward what you love—and again, that might not be your strong suit.

Finding your style could take months, especially if you are taking lessons once a week. Be patient and enjoy the ride.

How I found my musical style

When I was in your shoes, yo, I tried everything to find my musical style. I tried jazz, classical, R&B, pop, rock, urban, country and yes, even folk music—everything known to man. I played pop and rock. I joined jazz, country and R&B bands. I did everything I could to throw myself into those styles.

When I wanted to learn about pop music, for instance, I said, "I'm going to buy every pop record out there and study them all. I'm only going to listen to the pop station for the next three months." I'd be in my room or in my mom's car listening to the radio trying to really understand what the Doobie Brothers meant to me and if I could feel any passion connected with them. I was a kid who was into James Brown, R&B, Motown and a little bit of the Beatles, so when I first heard rock stars like Led Zeppelin and Jimi Hendrix, I was like, "Whoa. This is some different stuff here." The more I listened to it, the more I loved it.

Then I asked myself, "Yo Dawg, is this me?" I'd watch TV to see what the stars did. See how they hung out, what they wore, how they moved on stage, how the music made them feel. You should do this too, to see if a particular style suits you. If you could see yourself doing this. Can you see yourself as more of a Mick Jagger or Steve Tyler, prowling around on stage? Do you vibe like them? Can you see yourself as someone like Gwen Stefani, cooing into the mike? Or someone like Lauryn Hill, giving it to them straight? Can you see yourself as someone as bold as Prince, back in the day when he wore a trench coat, G-string, high-heeled boots, a big cross and a lot of makeup?

After trying out all kinds of music, I zeroed in on jazz fusion. Cats like Miles Davis and John Coltrane inspired me. This is what struck a nerve with me. I also picked jazz fusion because I was trying to become the ultimate technical musician—able to play anything. Jazz fusion to me is the hardest music to play. You have to be so proficient on your instrument. Playing five tempos at the same time, for instance. I wanted to try the toughest music because I knew if I could do that, I could do anything.

Later on in my career, I picked pop R&B as my style, so I could play to a wider audience. Music for the masses. Not so specialized, like jazz fusion.

So what's your deal? To find out what your musical style is, you can ask yourself:

- Are you more like Whitney Houston or Justin Timberlake, who sing pop R&B?

- Are you more like Sheryl Crow, who sings folky rock?

- Are you more like 50 Cent or Missy Elliott, who sing hip-hop?

- Are you more like Celine Dion and Britney Spears, who sing straight pop?

- Are you more like All-American Rejects and Maroon5, who sing alternative rock?

- Are you more like Faith Hill or Brad Paisley, who sing pop country?

- Are you more like Bruce Springsteen or the Foo Fighters, who sing rock?

- Are you more like Tool or Mudvayne, who sing hard rock?

- Are you like Audioslave, a post-grunge band?

If you don't like the style everyone is suggesting for you, you're going to have to "trial and error it" more to try and convince people that another style is better for you. But I'll tell you. We all have natural talent. Something we're good at without really trying. The thing to do is try and find out what that is, and capitalize on that. Work that, baby.

Immerse yourself

ONCE YOU FIND OUT WHAT YOU'RE BEST AT, here's where the real work begins. Listen to all kinds of records in that style so you become an expert on this type of music. You want to find out who is the best and how they got that way.

Ask your teacher to help you focus in on this style. Ask your teacher—what should I be working on vocally? What kind of music should I be singing? Do I sound like a pop or R&B singer yet? If not, what should I do to sound like one?

You also have to start thinking, if you had a shot at a career in this kind of music, what would you want to do? How would you be different? Why would somebody want to buy your records when they have so many others to choose from?

You'll never be as good as the Picasso

AT THIS STAGE, YOU CAN BECOME A COPYCAT for life. You may decide that you want to study Norah Jones' sound and music. But by immersing yourself in her sound and emulating her style, you can end up sounding exactly like her for life. Remember, you'll never get the best job this way because fans will always go for the original. As I like to say, you'll never be as good as the Picasso.

You'll know you're a copycat when all your friends say, "You know, you sound just like Christina Aguilera." Don't get all full of yourself when you hear that. Take that as a dig, like, "Yo, man, come on. I don't want to sound like somebody else. I want to sound like *me*."

You are trying to learn from others who have perfected a particular musical style. You used their records and songs to learn from at the beginning. But if you start sounding exactly like Beyoncé, Fred Durst, Justin Timberlake or 50 Cent, then stop! That's when you know you have your work cut out for you.

"Check and balance" yourself and stop listening to that artist. Obviously you've listened to them enough. If you catch yourself singing their runs, mimicking their gestures or copying their phrasing, then it's time to put those records away. Get your teacher to help you turn yourself around. You have to say, "Whoa, whoa, whoa. What am I doing here? Yo, what's up with this?"

Remember—you have to stay true to yourself. At the end of the day, you are selling you. That will help take you to the top.

Jay-Z is a good example of that. He has never changed who he is and has had a super successful career in hip-hop.

straight outta da Dawg's Mouth*—tip 10*

Sometimes when singers become overnight sensations, they feel overly confident. They think, "The public loved my pop album. It was number one on the *Billboard* charts for seven weeks. So they'll love everything I do." Then they completely switch styles with their next records—and fall flat on their faces. Remember, Dawg, the public only buys what the public believes to be true and honest.

Understanding music

AT THIS STAGE, YOU SHOULD BE "SPONGING AND learning" —soaking up everything you can about music, artists and the music industry. Sure you know Alicia Keys' and Ashanti's songs by heart. You know all the songs on *Billboard*'s Top Fifty. But you also need to broaden your perspective and learn about other great music—songs and artists that can enrich your career.

Here are a few of my recommendations. I have provided a much longer listening list in the back of the book. If you don't know who some of these people are, go to the library or to the music store and get some of their albums. Then just sit back and listen—over and over—and learn. There is something to be learned from everything.

■ **ARETHA FRANKLIN:** If you're a singer, you have to listen to the Queen of Soul. She is, to me, one of the most gifted singers of all time. You can learn so much from her unbelievable tone and the unending passion and spirit with which she sings. It's like being in the gospel church itself.

■ **STEVIE WONDER:** For me, probably the greatest of all time. He's beyond talented as a singer and musician. He can teach you about perfect pitch. He has a ridiculous sense of phrasing. He has an incredible sense of rhythm and note selection. He has an uncanny sense of runs. And he's a truly gifted songwriter.

■ **SHIRLEY MURDOCK:** You can learn how to sing with feeling from her. How to put your heart and soul into the music—something you definitely need to do if you want to make it in this business. Listen to her song "As We Lay" to hear how well she does it.

■ **MICHAEL JACKSON:** You can learn about phrasing from him because the phrasing he uses in his songs is impeccable. He is also the king of the uptempo song. You can learn how to sing fast songs from him.

■ **THE BEATLES:** You can learn about melody from the Beatles. The melodies in their songs were just phenomenal. Their lyrics were dope. What a picture they painted.

■ **MOTOWN:** You can learn about ballads, mid- and uptempo songs from some of Motown's biggest stars including the Supremes, Marvin Gaye and the Temptations. Motown had a unique way of putting music and melody together.

■ **AL GREEN:** He typifies soul. You can learn so much about passion from him.

Understand, you see a lot of older names here because most of the younger stars you probably know and love learned from the greats, as I hope you do.

Passion, baby, passion

ANY TIME *IDOL* 2 WINNER RUBEN STUDDARD GOT up on stage and sang, his attitude was infectious. You fell in love with the glow on his face. His ear-to-ear grin. The feeling you got from him was, "I don't care what happens. I'm having the time of my life right now. I love this, and I hope that you get a sense of euphoria from it as well." You felt like his heart and soul were smiling and that was what people felt when they watched him. That's one of the reasons he won.

Eric Clapton's original version of "Layla" is what they could teach in Passion 101. In his guitar riffs you can hear his torment over the woman he lost. He is a master who learned how to convey emotion with his guitar from Muddy Waters and a lot of the old blues greats.

B.B. King can create a fire in your soul with one note, like in his song "The Thrill Is Gone." Nat King Cole did it with the sound of his voice, which moved you. So did Frank Sinatra's.

You have to learn to get that emotion across to the listener. You have to connect the passion you feel in your soul to your music, so it will come out when you sing or play. The public connects with singers and musicians who can convey what they're feeling in a genuine way. Remember Kelly Clarkson singing "A Moment Like This" on *Idol* 1's season finale? Now that was passion.

This is the reason that the young and the old love the blues. The blues are about connecting with someone else's soul. You want that soul connection, baby.

Whether you're playing a guitar solo or singing the national anthem, people need to feel your delivery, otherwise your performance will feel stale. Flat. Put it this way. If somebody on stage seems to be having the time of his or her life and is passionate about what he or she's doing and is conveying that to people, you kind of get turned on, don't you? But you have to make sure you're conveying that passion to the audience. You may think you're singing with passion, but it may not be coming across. You need infectiousness to draw people to you. Do you have that infectiousness?

One surefire way to find passion if you don't think you have it

FOR A CRASH COURSE IN PASSION, YOU MAY want to check out gospel music. Whether you're singing it or just listening to it, it can teach you so much. It's a great way to connect with your inner passion and to get real with your soul. It also gives you the chance to sing for something real. To sing for the love of music. When you're singing in a church choir or in church, you're singing for God and you're sharing a gift that God gave you. It allows you to sing for something other than money or fame.

From time to time, you'll hear me say on the show, "Oh, you're a PK," meaning a preacher's kid. I'll say, "With that kind of fire and passion in your delivery, I could tell that you grew up in the church. It's almost like you felt every word you sang."

Many singers we admire got their start in the church. Whitney Houston got her start in the gospel church, where her mother, Cissy, sang. I guess you could say Whitney's singing to the heavens helped her connect with her passion and her music. But then again, she was surrounded by music. Her mother, who was a member of the vocal group the Sweet Inspirations, sang backup for Aretha Franklin, a close friend of the family. Whitney would go with her mother to the studio for recording sessions. So she's four years old and she's sitting in the studio while her mom is singing with Aretha Franklin. Can you imagine growing up listening to that, coupled with her amazing talent and her work ethic? Oh my God, what an influence that is.

Stevie Wonder also sang and played piano in the church. God took away his gift of sight, but look at the amazing gift of music that he was given. He wrote the book on singing with passion and spirit. That's what you want to do.

So keeping this in mind, it might be a good idea to check out a church choir, so you can try and get in touch with that uplifting feeling of singing for the Most High. Try to understand what that feels like. Does it feel right to you? You can even sing along to a few records at home. Remember, with this and with anything else, you learn by doing.

Here are a few gospel singers I recommend listening to. These are some of the best gospel singers on the planet, who sing only with their hearts. You can learn a lot about style, passion, grace and technique from them.

Elements of their singing may pique your curiosity and you may want to use some of them when developing your own style. You may want to sing songs from these artists in your warm-up exercises. They'll rev you up.

- The Clark Sisters

- Fred Hammond and Commissioned

- Vanessa Bell Armstrong

- *The Bobby Jones Gospel Hour* (on BET)

- Sandi Patti

- Jaci Velasquez

- Kirk Franklin

- Andraé Crouch

- The Winans

- Ann Nesby

- Donnie McClurkin

- Kim Burrell

In the fan club

ALWAYS REMEMBER, DUDE, ADMIRATION FOR OTHERS CAN DRIVE your own ambition. Not that you want to become clones of the stars you think are hot—you shouldn't want to become anyone but yourself. But as you're beginning to develop your own style, it's good to believe so much in something that it inspires you to try harder and to work harder.

Say you love the Beatles. You think John Lennon is amazing. You may say, "He drives me every day. He inspires me."

Every one of us has a favorite artist who just juices us up. I'm a pretty even-tempered guy. I meditate twice a day. But if I'm ever down and out, which is rare, I put on some Sly and the Family Stone or, from my own home state, the Funky Meters—I love to play their "Hey Pocky Way." It's so dope and so honest and so full of raw passion that it lifts my spirits. They just have a joy of playing music that comes through in the song. That's what I love about it. So anytime you need inspiration or feel like the road is getting too tough, listen to the artists you admire, think of the journeys they were on—and keep going.

You want to make songs your own

ALL THE GREAT SINGERS, FROM GLADYS KNIGHT AND Mariah Carey to Celine Dion and Ella Fitzgerald, say, "Now that I've learned a song, let me take this melody and make it my own. Let me put my own spin on it." I saw that firsthand when I worked in Detroit recording a version of the Rolling Stones hit "Jumpin' Jack Flash" with Aretha Franklin, Keith Richards, Ron Wood and Steve Jordan for the soundtrack to Whoopi Goldberg's movie *Jumpin' Jack Flash.*

Aretha wanted to make this song her own. First she rehearsed at home. When she got to the studio, she sat at the piano and practiced what she was going to do. Don't forget, this was a legendary Rolling Stones hit. A trademark song of theirs. She wanted to put her stamp on it and bring something different to it. And she did. The song turned out to be unbelievable.

Embracing the Top Ten

AT THIS POINT IN YOUR CAREER, YOU SHOULD be just going crazy with music. You're learning about the greats. You're trying out different styles. You've found new artists you love. But one of the most important things you can do to get to the top is to learn how to embrace the Top Ten. Understanding it can help your career. Analyzing it will help you learn what and what not to do when trying to find those elusive hit songs you'll need later on to land a record deal—and make you a star.

Legendary producer Tom Dowd once told me, "Randy, if you're a budding producer, musician or singer/songwriter, you must first understand the Top Ten. You must figure out why the songs in the Top Ten are there and why those songs work." I told this to Capitol Records president Andy Slater, who said this is one of the best pieces of advice anyone could give someone on the way up.

Every song in the Top Ten is different. You can have a hip-hop song, a pop song, an alternative song, a country song and an R&B song on the list—all at the same time. The Top Ten could be comprised of stars like Beyoncé, Nelly, 50 Cent, Pharrell, R. Kelly, Brad Paisley, Kenny Chesney and Matchbox Twenty—all at once. You have to figure out why people have gravitated toward all those records. This was a big lesson to me.

The Top Ten on the *Billboard* charts or anywhere else means that these are the most popular records in the country that are bought, downloaded, listened to and requested on the radio, *right now*.

How can this help you? Well, you want to be a recording artist or a musician. You want people to like you and buy your albums. You want your music to be successful. So you need to start learning what people like and why. There's a common thread that runs through all types of hit songs that people connect with. You have to find out what the secret is to all these songs.

I may be some hip-hop kid living in the 'hood in Detroit who may say, "Why do I need to know anything about country music? Who cares?" You *should* care if a country song is in the Top Ten. You have to understand the who, what and why of it all. There is something very important to be learned here.

You can analyze the Top Ten by listening to the songs over and over. What I did when I was analyzing the Top Ten was to ask other people why they liked a particular song on the list. I would ask, "Why do you like Johnny Cash? What do his songs do for you?" His fans would say they liked his lyrics and the stories he tells in his songs. You can do the same and learn a lot to help boost your career.

I'll give you one tip. At any given time, you'll find that the artists who have made it to the Top Ten are true to themselves and their own musical style. Brad Paisley is a country guy. He loves being a country guy. He's not a country singer who's saying, "I wish I was like Jay-Z." No, that's not happening. You don't see Jay-Z or 50 Cent saying, "Yo, man. I like what I do, but I want to be Coldplay." People are buying 100 percent of who that person is.

But let's keep it real here. No lies. These people also have a hit song in their pocket. Memorable songs that grab you.

So, before we move on, always remember to let music be your guide. Let it lead you to your true soul salvation. Can I get an Amen? Ya'll know I need a witness, yeah...

Trying to Become a Big Dawg and Taking It to the Next Level

chapter four

SO, DUDE, YOU'VE BEEN PRACTIC-
ING LIKE CRAZY AND listening to all
kinds of music, soaking up everything you can. You've been spending time figuring out the right musical style for your vocal range and personality. Now you have to push yourself to
go even further to get to the next level.

At this stage, you have to refine the skills you've developed so far and constantly challenge yourself. This
includes playing gigs and performing. Yes, Dawg, this
means getting up in front of a real, live audience—not necessarily friends or family—and singing your heart out. You
have to take this step to get your groove on, so let's go.

Always push yourself to improve

ONE OF THE RULES I'VE FOLLOWED SINCE THE beginning of
my career is to constantly find new ways to challenge

myself. I've had a great time in the music business and have had amazing things happen to me. But I never look back. I don't keep awards I've received all over my house so I can sit and stare at them all day. I'm always looking forward. And so do a lot of the stars I work with.

I saw firsthand how Justin Timberlake stretched himself to go further than a lot of people thought he could when he produced a song I played bass on for *NSYNC's 2001 *Celebrity* album.

I remember walking into Westlake Studios in Los Angeles at about 6 P.M. the night we were working together. He and the band had been recording all day. As the producer, Justin was trying to make the song we were recording more urban with the bass lines I was playing.

For a pop band like *NSYNC, this was a departure—a way for them to reach new heights with their music. Keep in mind that crossing over from the pop side of the fence to the urban side is challenging for *any* artist. It's a total stretch. But they did it.

As the producer, Justin was just challenging himself, seeing how far the group could take what they were doing. You could feel him heading to that new place. He was feeling his weight in it. He was like, "I could really go there. I could really do this." The song turned out to be incredible. This album was nominated for a Grammy Award for Best Pop Vocal Album in 2002.

This is an example of a hugely successful star who was willing to stretch himself. Willing to test his limits, test his boundaries, and move the boundaries, if need be. He stretched himself even further when he went on to record his first solo album, *Justified*, later that year.

Like Justin, you can't ever be afraid to test your boundaries. The only way to know that something doesn't work for you is to try it. But you want to try it around people who are qualified to be able to tell you whether it worked or not and why. People who won't gas you and will tell you honestly, "Yo, you know, that ain't happening." Or "You know, you're busted on that." Remember to always keep it real, baby.

Bring it to the people

SO YOU'VE BEEN IN YOUR BEDROOM, RAPPING TO every Nelly and Eminem song they ever made. You've been singing every one of Alicia Keys' and Whitney Houston's songs in your teacher's music studio. And yo, you're trying to dress like all of them put together.

Now the time has come for you to polish your skills in front of the public. You need a captive audience so that you can show people on a regular basis what you've got. Not singing at open mike night to test the waters, like you did in Chapter 2. Now you're going to come out and see if people actually like to hear you play or sing.

Since you've chosen your musical style, you know which direction you're heading in. You know:

■ The kind of music you'll be singing or playing. If you're a pop singer, for instance, you could join a Top Forty band. If you play the guitar, you could join a rock or alternative band. If you play R&B bass, you can join an R&B or hip-hop band.

■ The kind of people you should be hanging out with, musically. If you like alternative music, for example, you want to primarily hang out with people who like alternative music too, not people who like country.

■ The kind of people you should be networking with. Again, if you want to meet people in the pop world, you shouldn't be trying to work it in the opera world.

■ The kind of scene that you want to be in. You don't want to be hanging out in a country and western bar seven nights a week if you want to become a hip-hop artist.

So how do you find a band?

TO FIND A BAND THAT PUTS YOU IN front of the public on a regular basis, you're going to do the same thing you did to find a teacher. You're going to talk to as many people as you can to see if they know of a band that's looking for a singer or musician. You can look in your local newspaper. You can also find a band that you like and ask them if they need help. If so, tell them you want to audition. Keep in touch with them so that when they have an opening, you're the first one they're going to call.

You can also do what I did. When I was 16 or so, I was lucky enough to start playing local gigs, weddings and parties with a lot of older musicians because I wanted to "sponge and learn" from them. They had way more knowledge and wisdom than I did at the time. I always wanted to play with people who were far better than me so that I could learn. Sometimes when I played with people my own age, we were learning things at the same time and couldn't help each other. I hooked up with some older cats because I wanted to rise to the next level.

There's one thing I want to point out. If you're going to clubs and bars to meet potential band members or musicians to work with, always take a friend with you to watch your back. Be careful out there.

straight outta da Dawg's Mouth—*tip 11*

So you're singing and playing in a band you really like. You should try and play as many weddings, parties and events as you can. Don't even think about the money at this point. I can't tell you how many thousands of jobs I played where I got little or no money. But I did it for the experience. Every time you sing or play, you have the opportunity to improve. You're learning and growing. Each time you step on a stage, you're polishing your skills—and getting closer to your goal.

"Trial and error it" on stage

CONGRATULATIONS! YOU'RE NOW GETTING PRIMO, PRIMO, ON-THE-JOB training by singing or playing on stage. You should still be rehearsing two to four hours a day with your band or by yourself. You should still be taking lessons from your teacher. You're still doing all of the things we've been talking about to lay the groundwork for success.

But now you have a place where you play a couple times a week, where you can try out new things to see if they're working. Let's say you've been listening to Mary J. Blige, Faith Evans and Brian McKnight and heard them doing some incredible runs. You decide you're going to try singing those runs at your next couple of gigs.

The best thing about playing for a live audience? Instant feedback from the audience. They're going to clap, cheer, ignore you, fall asleep, boo or walk out while you're performing.

By performing live, you can see if you're doing something right or wrong or if they like you, love you or could care less. You can see firsthand if you should continue trying to make it in the music business. Ultimately it's about you conveying your musical prowess to the public and the public paying money for that talent—buying your records, going to see your shows and concerts, listening to you and requesting you on the radio.

You'll also get feedback from your bandmates, especially if they're more experienced. They'll tell you, "Yo, man. That was dope." Or, "Don't do that anymore. That was horrible. That sucks."

Don't get all bummed out and defensive if some criticism comes your way. It's good that they're keeping it real with you. Now you know that you have to practice those runs or rework the way you tried that bridge. Or they may suggest doing something another way. This may be something you've never heard of that works.

Other people can also help you keep it real in other ways. You may think that you rocked the house when you rapped 50 Cent's "P.I.M.P.," but after the gig's done, no one mentions that song. Everyone in the joint tells you that you got off on Usher's "You Got It Bad." This tells you that maybe your objectivity is off a little bit and that you might need to refine it more.

You should also learn how to pace yourself on stage. A song should be played like a great movie, with a beginning, middle and end. You don't need to sing or play every lick or run you know in one measure. String these out. Stars usually save the pyrotechnics for the end of the song.

Get to know the tools of the trade

NOW THAT YOU'RE SINGING OR JAMMING IN FRONT of an audience, you need to make sure that you master the tools of your trade. If you're a singer, you have to learn how to perform with a microphone. You can ask your teacher to help you pick out the right one. You can "trial and error it" to find the right mike. Work with your teacher on mastering mike techniques.

If you're a musician, your main tool, of course, is the instrument you've been playing. Try to buy the best instrument you can afford until you can get an even better one.

Whether you're a singer or a musician, you can learn how to avoid feedback—that high-pitched screeching you hear when someone puts the mike too close to the speaker. Learn how to avoid it and how to fix it.

You should also learn how to use audio enhancers or effects processors to make you sound as good as you can while you're doin' your thing live or recording in the studio. Here are just a few of the audio enhancers you can use:

■ **REVERB:** This is the echoing that makes you sound so good when you sing in a tiled bathroom or in a concert hall. You can do this electronically with a reverb device, which can make the most of your voice or instrument.

■ **HARMONIZER (SOUND DOUBLER):** This gives your voice a different color, shape or tone. If you have a thin voice, you could use a Harmonizer to make your voice sound doubletracked—like there are two of you singing—or create a slight harmony with yourself.

■ **EQUALIZER:** Like the equalizer in your car or home stereo, you can use EQ—or equalization—to add or subtract bass, mid and treble when you're singing or playing live or in the studio. An equalizer helps control tone by playing up or playing down certain frequencies.

■ **COMPRESSOR:** This puts a squeeze on your voice or the music, to help to even out the soft and loud spots.

■ **DELAY:** This is a repeat effect on your voice or instrument, as though you were in a canyon yelling hello and you hear, "Hello, hello, hello, hello…" echoing back to you.

These are just a few of the tricks and effects you can use. But don't use these as a crutch. They're just there to enhance your sound.

If you don't know how to read music, you should ask your teacher to help you. A lot of people play by ear, which means they don't know how to read the notes. Learning to sight-read takes discipline, which will help you throughout your career. You can master anything you put your mind to. Knowing how to sight-read will open up many more job opportunities to you. If you can sight-read, you don't have to limit yourself to playing in a mediocre three-or-four-chord rock band for the rest of your life.

Remember, the person who shows up with all the right info has the best shot at the prize.

Jammin' in public has its perks

YOU NEVER KNOW WHO YOU'RE GOING TO MEET while you're out there playing. That's how Tori Amos got her entrée into the business. When I was working with Narada Michael Walden, he would always talk about this unbelievable girl who sang and played in the piano bar at a D.C. hotel where he liked to stay. He would talk about her strong voice and her talent on the keyboard. And he loved her energy.

So he flew her out to San Francisco to meet with our team. She didn't get her big break for two more years. But her meeting with us was one of the first steps she took to get out of the piano bar and really go for it.

You, too, can play in a piano bar or a cocktail lounge or a happening club and get discovered or find like-minded people who may help you along the way. It doesn't matter where you play, so long as you play the hell out of it. It's all about networking, meeting people, working it and showing people just how good you are.

Every time I'm in a hotel and I see a band playing in the lounge, like I used to do, I'll check it out. You never know where you're going to find the next big stars. And you never know who's listening. Don't think that people aren't.

Confidence—the double-edged sword

CONFIDENCE IS PRIMO FOR MAKING IT IN THIS business. But confidence isn't the whole story. You can have all the confidence in the world, but you aren't going anywhere if you aren't keeping it real, man. It's really about trying to be honest with yourself and getting to that place where you are really accepting of the challenge ahead of you.

Yes, you need confidence to help you stay in the game. But you really have to be able to accept the challenge and say, "I'm not that great. But I'm vowing to be the best. I'm not going to let them see me sweat. I'll do my own sweating on my own time, but I'm going to get it together and find out what great is and what's going to help me. I'm going to do it."

One of the biggest pitfalls at this stage is thinking you're ahead of the game when you're not. You may think you're the bomb now. It's easy to do. You're playing twice a week and you're getting paid for it. So dude, here is where Ms. or Mr. Ego starts whispering in your ear: "Yo, Dawg. You're the best. You don't need anybody else. It's you who's making all these people look good. It's because of you that people are coming to these shows."

All kinds of chicks and dudes start showing up and say to you, "Oh my God. You're so hot. You're incredible. When you sing, I get goose bumps. You're the best ever."

Then your friends and family show up at a gig where you rocked the house. After the show, your mama is crying because you were so good. Your cousins rally around you and say, "I didn't know you were that hot! You're the next Christina! You're the next John Mayer."

So now you say, "I've made it. I'm ready for a record deal."

Stop! You're not even close to being there yet. You're still in the development stages. You have to keep it real. You still have a lot to work on. You're still working on becoming the best you can be. Even though you may be good, you probably aren't anywhere near being the best yet.

You need to believe in yourself. That will help you to keep going in this tough, tough business. But never forget—you are training for the Olympics of music. You will be competing against THE BEST IN THE WORLD. You want to win. Keep practicing. Keep working on improving areas where you are weak.

But you have to balance confidence with conviction. You know, you definitely need to feel that you can achieve this, but you don't want to go overboard with the ego. You never want to think you're the best and that you can't learn anymore. Then you'll stop working and growing.

You always have to remember that you are a work in progress. And as I said before, always have humility. You don't have to flaunt your talent; people will get tired of you if you do. If you've got to prove it that hard, you must not have it. Then the ego becomes the thing that you're selling. You only want to sell your talent.

Ego can lead you astray. You want to stay focused. You may have family members and friends saying, "Oh my God, you're ready. You're incredible. You should go audition for that TV show. Why don't you have a record deal yet? What's wrong with you?"

You may also have would-be managers and others wanting to represent you and saying all kinds of things to you. "If you don't sign up now, you'll lose out forever." "I have a million people dying to work with me. If you don't take my offer, I'll just move on to the next wannabe."

Take a deep breath and remember, you have to stay true to yourself, no matter how hard it may be. If you know in your heart of hearts that you're not really ready, then don't take a step you may later regret. Don't let other people gas you up. Just tell them, "Yo, Dawg. I ain't ready yet. I got a lot more to do before I'm really, really ready. I'm trying to be the best. I can wait for mine."

Learn to trust your intuition. It will help you make better decisions. Seek advice from others. Listen to what the professionals you trust tell you. But in the end, always go with your gut. If something doesn't feel right to you, like making the decision to go for the big time now, then trust yourself.

It's like when you take a multiple choice test and as soon as you look at the question, you know the answer is B. But then you look at A and C and go back and forth and convince yourself that the answer is A, when it really was B all along. Trust your intuition. It won't fail you. And as I've said before, stay true to yourself.

The flip side of the confidence question

TOO MUCH CONFIDENCE CAN BE A PROBLEM. BUT so is a lack of it. If, by this point, you really doubt that you have what it takes to get up on stage and shake it or hang in there for the long haul, then maybe you should think about doing something else.

On *Idol* and here in this book, I don't want to burst anyone's dreams. I'm just trying to keep it real with you. At some point in your development, you've got to ask yourself, "Do I have it or don't I?" You have to keep asking yourself and professionals you trust along the way if you have what it takes.

Maybe you just need to go back and retrace your steps and try something a little different. But if you still can't find the wherewithal to do this, it's OK. No one is forcing you to do this. No one is saying you have to be a singer or musician.

Thickening that skin

IF YOU DO DECIDE TO HANG IN THERE and you're performing in front of an audience, you have to start developing that thick skin I told you about in Chapter 1. Now that you're standing up there on stage, all kinds of things can happen.

You may get standing ovations and make everyone cry with joy. You may also hear things you don't want to. Imagine what they said about Mick Jagger when he was first starting out. "He's so skinny. He's got such big lips!" Everything you can think of.

The audience isn't there to love you yet. They may extend common decency with light clapping, but that's about it. But think about it. They don't know you at this point. So they're asking, "Why should I pay my money to hear you sing? What are you gonna sing about?" Remember, dude, the public wants simple things. They want to enjoy themselves and like what they're hearing.

One way to develop that thick skin is to believe in yourself. Just look at Clay in *Idol*'s second season. He was a brilliantly talented singer but one of the geekiest-looking kids to audition. He may have doubted at first whether he would end up with a record deal. He made it into the Top 32 but was eliminated. But when we brought him back for the Wild Card portion of the show for another shot at the prize, that's when I feel he really started believing in himself. That he could really do this. He knew he had the voice, he knew he had the talent and that's why he showed up. People voted him in and he won the Wild Card. He ended up coming in second, just behind Ruben. He now has fans all over the world who go crazy for him. He's definitely doin' his thing.

Same thing with Ruben. He, too, believed in himself and won. He, too, has millions of fans and a promising career. He's gettin' it done.

Remember, good things happen when you start believing in yourself.

Still working hard?

I HATE TO TELL YOU THIS, BUT IT'S still not time for chillin'. As I've said, making it in this business is hard work. Making an album takes most artists three months to a year—or more. That's a long time. You have to go through a lot of songs. You have to perfect them. You have to record them and get them ready for release.

Mariah Carey is a star who is known for her work ethic and punishing schedule. When you're working with her in the studio, 14-hour days are the norm. Dinner breaks are quick. Why? Because she is working in the moment. She is striving to be the best, always, to give her fans the best.

The same thing with Madonna. When you are working in the studio with her, she's like, "Let's go. Let's go. Let's keep going." She's really focused on what she's doing and what she's trying to accomplish.

When Bruce Springsteen is working on an album, he's in the studio every day. He's concentrating and thinking, "How can we make this better?"

All of these people can sing anything backward and forward. But they want to give the best performances they can. And that takes work. They're also trying to make sure that the songs they're creating connect with the listener emotionally. It's not just about making a song mechanically correct. When Whitney sings the words "I believe in you and me," it's about getting that emotion across. When you sing it, does the listener believe that you believe in you and me?

straight outta da Dawg's Mouth—*tip 12*

Nobody said this was going to be easy. Practicing every day. Singing on stage night after night. Hoping for that big break. Dude, believe it or not, the struggle you're facing today is going to be one of the best things for you when you look back years from now. It's what's going to help you stay humble and respect how you got to where you are. And that's what's going to help keep you there. You won't take your success for granted because you'll remember how hard it was for you to get there. As the old saying goes, nothing worth having comes easy.

straight outta da Expert's Mouth

Here is an interview with my girl Nikka Costa, a dope singer I manage. She has a successful career, but knows all about how hard it is to make it in this business.

RANDY: So Nikka, talk about how you came up.

NIKKA: I grew up in the business. My father, Don Costa, was an arranger, composer and producer. He worked a lot with Frank Sinatra. He arranged and produced "New York, New York" and "My Way."

I made a couple records when I was a kid and then took a break. When I graduated from high school in Los Angeles, I decided I really wanted a career in music. So I started writing my own songs, and became very hands-on about what kind of artist I wanted to be.

I think it's really important to write your own songs. I had a voice and I wanted to share the thoughts that I had, so I started writing. When I had a couple songs written, I wanted to sing with a band. I was in Sydney, Australia, at the time. I would go check out bands around town, anything from Led Zeppelin and Sly and the Family Stone cover bands to other young groups around town, trying to find funk and rock players for the band I had in mind.

I also tried different instruments. I'm certainly not a great guitarist or pianist or anything, but I can string some chords together, which is all I needed to write songs. You don't need to be a virtuoso player to write songs.

I formed a band and I booked gigs, starting in tiny venues, wherever anyone would take me, because nobody knew me yet. But I had a pretty clear idea of what I wanted to do. What style I loved. Then I just went out and toured. I got a van. I put up my own posters. I drove the van and the band across Australia, touring.

I kept playing gigs, got some attention and got signed in Australia. I made a record and toured all over Australia and New Zealand. Then I decided to move back to America to try making it there.

And then I had to do the same thing all over again! I got a band together. I wrote songs and played around Los Angeles. I got signed with Virgin Records and had a record out in 2001—*Everybody Got Their Something.* I had a pretty good run. I was nominated for Best New Artist in a Video at the MTV Music Awards for that album. Now I'm making a second record for Virgin.

RANDY: What advice do you have for people just coming up?

NIKKA: Get a demo together if you're trying to land gigs. Most venues will want to at least hear what you can do if they've never heard of you before. Then they can see if they like you and can put you in the right lineup. If you're brand-new, you'll probably be playing at six at night in front of no one, or three in the morning in front of no one. But then you just start building a name for yourself, you get to know the venue owners and keep going.

Hopefully, if you're any good, the buzz around town will grow to the point where labels start getting interested in you and start coming to your gigs.

You can either wait for a label to sign you, or you can go independent, build your act, record your own CD and sell it on the Internet or at gigs.

Get educated about your rights as an artist and your contracts. As boring as that all seems, and is, know who gets what, and know what you're signing before you sign anything.

Always stay true to the kind of music you love. Audiences can read when you're faking it, or when you're doing something that you think people want you to do.

At the end of the day, you have to persevere more than anything. Don't give up. Write, collaborate and play, play, play.

If you start to lose steam

Always remember, you are doing this for the love of the game—music. To be in this game, you have to love it, because it's a very hard game. If you ever start to lose your drive, put on one of those gospel records I told you to listen to in Chapter 3 or play some B.B. King or Muddy Waters.

Listen to the passion that these people are singing and playing with. These people loved the music. They should help bring you back down to earth and remember why you are in this. You can't work this hard if you don't love the game. And as you progress, you should be developing the work ethic you will need for the rest of your career. Without that, it will all end in a bust . . .

Where to go from here?

WHAT IS YOUR DREAM JOB? TO LAND A deal with a major label? To join a hot band? What's it going to be? Now that you've been working, you need to start thinking about where you're headed and what your career path should be.

What is your next goal? Say you've been doing this for a year or more. You've progressed. You started singing one night a week at a local club and now you're playing five nights a week. You still may need a couple years of this to be ready. But now you may start seeing some light at the end of the tunnel—way, way, way in the distance—and so now is a good time to pinpoint exactly what it is you want to do.

You can decide that "Hey, I want to get a major record deal as a solo artist," or "I want to be in a band and get a dope record deal," or "I want to do theater because that's really where my heart is, because I also may want to act and sing and dance."

Once you pinpoint where you want to head, you can start focusing your energies there. If you want to go for a record deal, then you'll need to make a recording demo and try to get it into the hands of someone at a record company. If you want to do musical theater, then you'll need to start auditioning for shows.

If you're in a hip-hop or alternative band, you may want to record your own CD and sell it on your own. If you start developing a big following, record companies may pick up on that.

So you have lots more to work on. We're still not done yet . . .

Mirror, Mirror on the Wall
... How to Work with What Your Mama Gave Ya

chapter five

YOU GO TO THE MOVIES AND SEE BEYONCÉ, looking oh-so-fine in *The Fighting Temptations*. You see Gwen Stefani, rolling around on a bed in her sexy video "Underneath It All."

You spot Britney on the cover of *Esquire* magazine wearing a curve-hugging white sweater and nothing else.

You begin to think, "This is what I need to look like to make it."

I believe America is the most sensationalized country in the world. Everything, it seems, is about looks. Which diet shaves off the pounds the fastest? What's the best workout? Should I get plastic surgery?

There's no getting around it. Everywhere we turn—TV, movies, commercials, print ads, music videos, billboards— we see hot-looking models, actors, actresses, singers, etc. with seemingly perfect *everything*.

You begin to wonder: "Do I even need to sing or do I just need to get my look goin' on?"

A lot of people in the record industry look like models. But then again, many don't. And that is what I want to share with you. In the music industry, looks don't matter as much as you think if you have talent and a great song.

Case in point: Ruben and Clay. Ruben is a big guy. No question. He could have weighed one thousand pounds but *nobody cared* because when that boy sang, he made you forget all that. Baby, he had that chill factor goin' on.

And yo. When Clay came into the audition with his glasses and his big ears, he sure didn't look like what the industry would call a star. But we didn't care, because his pipes brought the house down.

It all boils down to this: The perception that you had of them was that they were beyond talented. It wasn't about how they looked.

The mirror is your best friend right now because it's a good way to see what you're really working with. The mirror will help you enhance your look, but will also help you see how you look when you're singing. Do you make funny faces when you hit the high notes? Looking your best can certainly help you, but ultimately, it's about the voice.

Don't forget about persona

SOME OF THE BIGGEST STARS AROUND TODAY AREN'T known for their looks. It was their "it" factor and their *personas* that made it happen for them. The definition of persona in Dictionary.com is "The role that one assumes or displays in public or society; one's public image or personality, as distinguished from the inner self." Persona is important.

Look at Mick Jagger. I'm sure he got clowned in school for having big lips. But you know what? He has an amazing persona. He also worked with what he had and now he's a supernova.

Barbra Streisand's nose is almost as famous as she is. She has never had a nose job. She embraced who she is. And you know what? So have millions of others. She has an incredible persona. She's a living legend.

When Jewel was starting out, people talked about her crooked teeth. You know what? It didn't matter. She's a huge star. She is a great example of someone who used what her mama gave her.

Dude, everyone you can imagine has flaws. Nobody is perfect. Even if you think they are, they're not. I always say there's no Christ—the perfect person—walking the planet. My girl, Nikka Costa, wrote a song about this very subject called "Everybody Got Their Something."

She's so right. But this doesn't stop the stars you admire. They keep going. In fact, they often turn negatives into positives. They joke about their big noses or crooked teeth. They show off their big lips. They play up their big butts. Look at how J-Lo worked her booty. It's all part of their aura. Their persona.

The funny thing is that once the public accepts that persona, they don't seem to notice the bountiful booty, the humongous honker or the supersize lips. They're too busy liking these people for who they are. And they even come to love those stars for those things. Crazy, right?

We saw this on *Idol*. The most gorgeous people didn't win. America voted for the talent, not the looks.

Workin' your aura

CREATING AN AURA OF SUCCESS, POWER OR TALENT will overshadow any faults you may have. Your aura is basically how people perceive and see you. You see it all the time. Let's say you're at Starbucks and someone walks in who commands attention. This person is confident. Open and friendly. Everyone in the room is drawn to this person. It's that magnetism I was telling you about.

You want to develop this as a performer. You want the public to like you. You don't want to turn people off as soon as you walk on stage.

You can convey that aura of success, power and talent if you truly love what you're doing, love singing and love the music. That's going to make the person sitting in the audience or listening to you on the radio love you, too. As I've said before, you're trying to get that soul connection, baby. You're trying to make people believe in you—and in your talent.

How do you do that? First, second and third: You've got to love who you are. That's the main thing. I don't care what size you are, what color you are, how tall you are or how big your nose is. Whatever. You've got to love your look and start "shakin' what your mama gave ya."

People talked about J-Lo. "She's got a big booty." So what? She made people *love* it.

People talked about Ruben. They'd say, "Man, he's huge. He's like a mountain."

His answer? "I don't care. You're going to love me because I love me."

Remember, it's really first about your talent and about loving yourself.

You have the power to change, if you feel you need to

THIS IS ABOUT PUTTING YOUR BEST FORWARD. YOU know if you have issues—problems with acne, weight loss or weight gain, or how you dress. Maybe you've dyed your hair so much that it's now crispy and fried. Maybe your dreads are out of control. Maybe your weave is just busted. If you want to change any of that, you've got the power.

I recently had gastric bypass surgery done by the renowned Dr. Mathias Fobi in Los Angeles to help jump-start my weight loss because I was getting to an unhealthy point in my life. I needed to lose weight once and for all. I tried everything but nothing stuck. When I was bigger, I felt like I was large and in charge. The good news? Even though I'm losing weight, I still feel large and in charge!

But at the end of the day, what it's really about is diet and exercise and, most important, about being healthy and accepting who you are. I'm not eating a fourth as much as I used to. And I'm working out every day. That's what's helping me. So if you have to work out every day and cut your eating from 5,000 calories to 1,500, do it. Do whatever it takes. Work it out.

You don't need stylists, makeup artist and trainers . . . yet

SO OFTEN WHEN PEOPLE ARE THINKING ABOUT CHANGING their look, they'll say to me, "I don't have the money those stars do to look really hot."

But guess what? Keeping it simple is one of the best things you can do for yourself. If you don't have the money to hire Beyoncé's hairstylist, then go another route. Nobody says you have to look just like her or Jessica Simpson or Kylie Minogue. In fact, I'm telling you NOT to look just like them.

The other thing is that most of these stars have teams of people who work on them—makeup artists, hairstylists, manicurists, masseuses, facialists, trainers, nutritionists and stylists to help them with their clothes. They've got the cha-ching to afford all this, so unless you have the same amount of cheddar in your bank account, you're not going to be able to compete on the same level. And you don't have to—yet.

Defining your look

OF COURSE, YOU DEFINITELY NEED YOUR OWN LOOK. When you're heading on stage for an audition or a performance, you need to look your best. You want to look polished, dude. You want to develop a great sense of style. You can do this by watching others. Really work it, the same way you're developing your talent. Put some effort into this. Check with some professionals—makeup artists or hairstylists at your local salon—to see if your look is right. Talk to people who work in clothes stores in your town. Tell them what you're doing. Ask for help with your overall look.

When you're trying on clothes, ask yourself and others, "Do I look good in this? Do I attract more attention when I'm wearing a suit or blue jeans and a T-shirt? A slinky black dress or short shorts and a halter top?"

Or you may say, "I want my makeup to look like Gwen Stefani. But when I wear a lot, do I look like Gwen or Marilyn Manson?"

Some people think they look good with a 'fro, but would be better off bald.

Just as you pinpointed the musical style that's right for you, you have to define your look. You might not always get it right at first. When I was growing up and trying out different looks I'd seen on TV, my dad, Herman Sr., would let me down easy by saying, "You know, son, style ain't for everyone," meaning not everyone could make this look work. Or I'd ask him, "Dad, do you think I look good?" and he'd stop and say, "On some level, everything is interesting."

Wow!

Just 'cause it looks good on Justin Timberlake or Ja Rule doesn't mean it will look good on you.

"Trial and error it" before you go with a look. And think about what's going to keep you unique. What's going to make you come across as you? What's going to strengthen your weaknesses?

But just don't go too overboard with it. Remember, a little goes a long way.

Killer looks that could kill a budding career

INCREDIBLY GOOD LOOKS CAN BE A DOUBLE-EDGED SWORD in this business. If you're ridiculously fine or a Denzel look-alike, sometimes you have to work harder to get people to focus on your talent, instead of your face or body. Looks alone aren't going to carry you in this business. You'll never know if you're being accepted or respected for your talent —or your beauty. When you are almost too gorgeous, people sometimes have the preconceived notion that you got where you are on your looks alone. That you can't really sing. So you really have to prove to them that you do have talent.

Attitude matters

YOU ARE WHAT YOU THINK. IF YOU THINK negatively, that's what the world will see. Check yourself before you wreck yourself, as I like to say. Ask yourself, "Am I the most negative person I know? Is it hurting me?"

As hard as this journey is, try to enjoy it. Keep positive affirmations in the forefront of your mind. That's what's going to draw people to you. Say to yourself, "I'm trying really hard to make it. I'm working every day. I'm going to really make a run for this. I'm going to learn everything I can. I know who I am."

Never tell yourself, "Oh my God, I'm already there," when you just started six months or a year ago. Don't gas yourself up, saying, "Oh my God, I'm the one. No one's better than me." Or "I see those stars on TV. I can do that. That's easy. I'm better than them."

That's not the kind of attitude you want to carry around. There will always be people better than you. Trust that. As soon as you say there's no one better than you, that's when someone shows up who is, and you say, "Wow. Who is *that?*"

You want to think about being the best you can be, without ego or delusions. End of story.

Reality, people, reality.

And yo, if you make mistakes, don't beat yourself up. Learn from them. Many spiritual people believe there are no mistakes in life, only lessons. I live by that. Now I know what not to do again . . . finally!

On stage

IF YOU'RE WORKING ON CREATING AND IMPROVING YOUR look and how others see you, then you should also think about how people see you on stage. Rehearse on stage and ask others for feedback. Work with the microphone. See what the audience likes and dislikes and work on that.

Watch and learn from other people. Maybe even take some dance classes, so you can learn how to move and dance better on stage—or just feel more comfortable up there. Nobody wants to watch somebody just stand there on stage. You need to be able to project and entertain people.

Be bold. It can go a long way toward helping you in your career. I remember one girl from Chicago who auditioned for *Idol*. She had a great voice, but was just too frightened. She seemed unable to come to grips with being overweight. That made her a shy person and hurt her in the end.

Let that personality come out. Whether you're fat, skinny, have big lips or no hair doesn't mean you've got to stand in the back and hide. Look at *Idol* 2 contestant Frenchie Davis. She wasn't a size 2, but had a voice as big as the Grand Canyon. Like Ruben and Clay. They didn't stand in the back. They pushed their way up front. They went for theirs. They said, "There's nothing that can stop me. I'm getting this." They did. And you can, too.

The all-important demo

SO DAWG, YOU'RE WORKING YOUR VIBE—HOW YOU look, how you come across to others and how you sound on stage. But at this point in your development, you also want to make sure you come across well on your demo—one of the most important ways you'll be presenting yourself to others.

A presentation demo is a CD demonstrating to others what you can do as a singer or musician.

Your demo is your calling card. Proof that you can sing or play. You can use it to find a band to join or musicians to work with. Later on, you can use it to help find a songwriter, manager or producer.

If you have a demo and you run into someone who might be able to help you, you can say, "I'm a singer. I'm very talented. I would love some help writing or producing some songs." Then you hand them the demo so they can check out your talent for themselves and see if you're someone they want to work with.

Hey, you may meet me, Randy Jackson, in an airport, in a store or in a restaurant and tell me you want to work with me. All kinds of people do it already. It's like I have a sign on my head that says, "Sing for me."

People have stopped me in bathrooms, at the car wash, the gas station, by the pool when I'm staying at a hotel and even in Barney's New York in Los Angeles while I was in the dressing room trying on pants, to sing for me and to see if I want to work with them.

I don't mind when people come up to me and show me their wares. I understand where they're coming from. They're just trying to get their groove on. I would do it, too.

Carpe diem, baby

IF YOU ARE PRESENTED WITH AN OPPORTUNITY, YOU have to *seize the moment*. No chickening out. No saying, "I'll do it next time." Dude, this opportunity may never come around again.

Case in point: A few months ago, I was flying to Atlanta to showcase a dope singer/songwriter I manage named Van Hunt, who's signed with Capitol Records. At the check-in counter at the airport, one of the girls there says to me, "By the way, I'm a singer." She starts talking about *American Idol.*

So I say to her jokingly, "Yo. Why don't you sing something right here at the counter?" I was basically saying to her, "Hey. I'm in the music business. If you're hot, if you're dope, let me hear you sing because I might want to help you if I'm really feeling you. So if you want to go for it, right now, here's your opportunity."

So she says, "I can't do that."

"OK. Cool."

So I went about my business and headed toward my gate. All of a sudden, the chick from check-in came racing toward me and started singing at the top of her lungs. The whole airport stopped to listen.

I said to her, "Yo. You know what? You probably *can* do this because the first thing that you showed me is that you are bold enough to get your groove on, no matter what, and take advantage of an opportunity on the spot."

Her voice was actually pretty good, but wasn't exactly what I was looking for, so I gave her some words of encouragement, told her to keep going and what to work on. Who knows where she may end up?

Seize the moment, dude. Seize the moment.

Knowing how to audition well can also help you get your career off the ground. One of my best buds, Barry Squire, an A&R consultant who specializes in musician referrals, can tell you all about auditioning. He teaches a musician audition workshop at the Musician's Institute in Los Angeles. He and I also have been co-teaching a class at the UCLA Extension School for the past nine years called "A&R: Acquisition to Release."

RANDY: So Barry, what advice do you have for people when they're auditioning?

BARRY: If you're auditioning for a band or as a background singer or musician for an artist, research the artist or the band to make sure that when you're at the audition, you're compatible with the artist. Know their background and style. Know the record companies they've worked with and the history of their music. Artists are looking to hire somebody who's compatible with their lifestyle. They can also interpret your knowledge about their music and background as enthusiasm for the project. This can help get you the job.

Learn the material as well as possible. You will have an advantage if you go to an audition and you have learned the song the way it was recorded. The artist will tell you if you can take liberties with the original arrangement or not. But it's impressive to come in and be able to play the song exactly as the artist recorded it.

Try and get the earliest audition time possible. Auditions tend to run late and wear down the parties involved, which can hurt you. You don't want to audition to a roomful of judges or artists who have been listening to musicians for five or six hours and are ready to go home. If you audition late, you also run the risk of not being able to perform at all because the organizers frequently overbook the amount of people they can accommodate in one day.

During the actual audition, try and make some kind of personal or eye contact with the judges or the recording artist or band you're auditioning for, even if it's just saying hello.

You can break the ice by knowing something about a common musical interest, the state they grew up in, or some past show they did that you admired. This is a way to leave a personal impression.

Sometimes the people holding the audition will ask you to send them a promotional package in advance so they can select the people for the audition. Make sure to have an organized promo package with a current photo with current information. One mistake people make is to reuse promotional materials with crossed-out contacts and phone numbers. This looks bad to prospective employers. It shows that your business relationships haven't been very stable.

Presentation demos versus recording demos

KEEP IN MIND THAT A PRESENTATION DEMO IS different from a more involved recording demo—the one you'll need later on when you're trying to score a record deal. Don't waste your time and money producing the most unbelievable piece of music anybody's ever heard for your presentation

Spend the extra money for fresh promotional material.

Don't overdo your promotional package. Most prospective employers don't have time to look through 20 or 30 pieces of paper. Don't include reviews that make you look dated—nothing that's more than three years old.

RANDY: Barry, what advice do you have for those who are trying to make it?

BARRY: To be successful as a musician or singer, it takes more than extraordinary talent. A musician or singer needs to know how to find work, and how to do well at auditions.

Treat your search for musical opportunities just like a regular job. Most successful musicians spend two or three hours a day networking with other musicians and following up on opportunities.

Try and go to as many auditions and jam sessions as possible. A lot of contacts are made interacting with musicians or singers waiting to perform.

Don't try and compete at an audition that's beyond your musical territory. Nothing is as embarrassing as a pop musician trying to fit in at a Marilyn Manson audition.

demo. You're not making records and you're not a producer yet, even if you think you are.

This is only a presentation to showcase your vocal or instrumental abilities. If you can really sing and really play, people should be able to hear that quickly and easily.

Some people may ask, wouldn't an eight-piece band make you sound better? You don't need all of that fanfare with a presentation demo. You only need to show that you can play or sing. This is not about the song or the production. It's a demo to get people interested in trying to do something with you.

What should be on your demo

FOR A PRESENTATION DEMO, YOU CAN SING COVER songs or original songs. If you're a singer, you may want to have an acoustic piano or acoustic guitar accompany your vocals, to highlight your voice. You can also sing along to some karaoke tapes. You could sing one song each from Mariah, Celine and Whitney to showcase your talent and range if you are a pop singer, for instance.

If you think you're a really dope singer, you can sing one of the songs a capella—without any musical accompaniment—and then maybe do one or two songs accompanied by a piano or guitar.

If you're in a band and you're an instrumentalist, you can perform solos, playing in three distinct styles for your demo. You could play blue grass, jazz and R&B funk, pop or some big ballads. If you play piano, you might want to play an acoustic solo.

Three's a charm

THERE IS NEVER A NEED TO PUT MORE than three songs on your demo. This is standard. Most people in power aren't going to listen to more than 10 or 15 minutes of a demo, if they make it that far. If they like what they hear, they could listen to all of it. If they don't, they'll listen for about one minute and turn it off, like I do when I get a demo that doesn't do it for me.

If you like, you can put your picture on the cover, *if* you have a picture that's great and shows you in your best light. Don't use a picture of you at your prom, on your high school basketball team or at your wedding. Trust me, I've seen every picture that you can imagine on the cover of a demo. You don't want people laughing at your picture. You want them interested enough to want to check you out. Remember, you are trying to put your best out there.

On the inside of the CD, put the names of the songs you're singing, along with your name, address, phone number and e-mail address. End of story. Keep it simple.

What about the cheddar?

MAKING A PRESENTATION DEMO SHOULDN'T COST AN ARM and a leg because this demo is simple. If you're doing this by yourself, or if someone is even helping you, it shouldn't cost a whole lot of money.

The biggest pitfall with making a presentation demo is someone overcharging you or getting too involved trying to make this a huge production.

If making a presentation demo sounds like too much money, it probably is. Shop around if you think the cost is too high. In life, you get what you pay for, but you don't need to pay a lot for this. Yet.

Where do you make a demo?

YOU CAN RECORD YOUR SONGS IN A STUDIO. You can look for a studio in any local trade paper or in the local newspaper. You can ask your teacher or go to any music store to find one. Employees at music stores in your town should know where you can find a studio that has a good sound engineer. They should also be able to tell you how much you can expect to pay.

Choose a musician to come and play with you. Practice your songs enough so that you can sing them in two or three takes. That way, you'll only need to be there for a few hours to record it and mix it. By keeping it simple and knowing your songs back and forth, you can save money. You don't want to waste time tinkering when you're at the studio. You want to go in there with one concept and stay focused.

The studio isn't the only place you can record a demo. You can also record a demo using your home computer or your laptop computer. You can use a hard disc-based digital recording system, such as Pro Tools, Logic Audio, Cubase, Digital Performer or Cakewalk (for IBM).

Using your computer, you can make your demo almost anywhere, from a home office to a garage. Most of the records that you hear today are recorded with the use of these kinds of computer programs, which have all kinds of editing features, plug-ins—or effects—and options. You can do anything imaginable in the recording process. Record live, record any instrument, and mix and edit to your heart's content.

Another option is going to a karaoke studio to record your presentation demo. Malls often have them. You go inside of a karaoke booth, and they'll record you singing well-known songs for not much money.

These are just some of the ways to record your demo. There are many other ways that you can find out about at your local music store or from one of the pros you're hopefully talking to.

Don't sign anything yet!

AT THIS POINT, SIGN NO CONTRACTS WITH MANAGERS, agents or producers. You're not ready for that yet. That comes later. Someone should want to work with you 'cause they're down—they think you're good. If they promise and threaten that they won't work with you unless you sign a contract with them, move on.

You want to keep it casual right now. You can say, "Hey, we can work together, but I'm not signing anything right now," or "Thanks, but I don't need a manager, lawyer, agent, producer right now. If you want to write some songs with me, or produce some songs with me or engineer some songs with me, fine, but we're gonna do it with no strings attached."

They may have no problem with that or they may get mad. Stick to your guns. Remember, as you make your way in this business, you're going to find people who always want to sign you up. People want to attach themselves to rising stars. Everyone's looking for the diamond in the rough because they know that at some point, the diamond will get polished. When it does, they want to be there.

Many artists on their way to the top have signed contracts they regretted later on. So dude, don't let anybody talk you into anything at this point in your career. As I said earlier, if something doesn't seem right to you, walk away. Stay strong. Because as you know, only the strong survive.

"Check and balance" yourself

WHILE YOU'RE NAILING DOWN YOUR LOOK AND HOW you're presenting yourself to the world, it's very important for you to record yourself once a week so you can hear what you sound like and chart your progress. It doesn't matter if you use an inexpensive tape recorder from Wal-Mart or a digital voice recorder. You're learning to develop your ear and hear what you sound like. You're using this as a mirror so that you can begin to tell honestly where you are and what you need to work on. It helps you hear how you sound to other people.

The recording demo

SO YO, LET'S SAY YOU THINK YOU'RE REALLY ready now. You think you're "it." That you're better than Dr. Dre, P.O.D. and Alien Ant Farm.

You think you don't need a presentation demo. You want to go for a record deal *now*. I personally think that's the wrong thing to do at this stage of your career. But dude, if you are among the persistent few (I hope) who insist on making your recording demo now, or if you've read through this entire book and have spent a lot of time preparing and think you really are ready now, here's what to do:

1. Find a great songwriter.

2. If that songwriter is not a producer, find a great producer.

3. Get your money together. You're going to need a lot of cheddar to make this a great demo if you're trying to get a record deal. A recording demo can cost anywhere from $3,000 to $12,000—maybe more or maybe less. That's because you'll need to pay the musicians, programmers, studio costs and maybe a producer.

Recording demos are serious business. People often spend much more than they anticipated on demos if things don't go as planned. And they usually don't. Making a recording demo is like building a house. You begin with one plan and then realize that you have to change gears. Shifting gears costs money. When making your demo, you realize that you might have to sing your song more times than you thought. You might need more musicians than you budgeted for. You might decide to hire the most expensive engineer in town because he's known to be the best.

Remember, you're trying to make the best product that you can at this point because you're trying for the Holy Grail—a record contract. Now is the time to "bring it" because you think you have it.

The truth is that many people do countless numbers of demos. I can't tell you how many demos I did before I was able to get someone to pay attention to me and get a record deal. I thought I was a primo musician. At that point, I had worked on more than 400 records as a session musician. I was a staff producer with Narada Michael Walden. I thought I knew it all and I *still* had to make 15 different demos to get people to notice me.

You're going to try to make the best demo you can make. And in the chapters that follow, I'll tell you how to get it into the right hands. But you may fail because so many elements have to work. Is the song right? Is the producer right? Is he or she getting the best performance out of you? Are you heading in the right direction? Will this demo make the cut?

When I was doing A&R, I would get about 100 CDs a week—most of them garbage. You need to be as good as Missy Elliott, the Goo Goo Dolls and all the other artists out there.

Why? All the record company wants to know is that you can make money for them. Welcome to the entertainment business. It's all about dollars and cents and how many units you can move. It's not about, "We like you. You're so nice. Let me give you a deal." No way.

It's not about how you tried hard with your demo. It's not about you spending all your money on this and it's not working. Save the tears and the whining for somebody else. No one cares. Unfortunately, success in the music business is measured in sales.

Song selection

IF YOU DECIDE THAT YOU'RE A BALLADEER à la Whitney Houston, then you might want to do two ballads and one up-tempo song. If you are going to focus on fast songs, à la Michael Jackson or Usher, you may want to do two up-tempo songs and one ballad. If you are a moody rock band like Coldplay, you could sing two of your moody rock songs and one that's really different.

This demo needs to be dope, dude. No ifs, ands or buts. It needs to compete with hits that are playing on the radio in your town. If not, try again next time.

Good luck finding that elusive hit

AS WITH THE PRESENTATION DEMO, YOU STILL NEED ONLY two or three songs on your recording demo. But here's the big difference: To make a killer demo, at least one of those songs needs to be a hit to catch the label's attention.

What's a hit song? A song that has an audience of more than 50 million people across the country. A song that radio stations *want* to play 300 times a day. A song that makes listeners jam the lines at radio stations trying to request that song.

But guess what? Hits, like stars, are the hardest thing in the world to find. If they were that easy to come by, every up-and-coming artist would be a multi-millionaire at this point, the record industry wouldn't be in a slump and people would be buying more records. Not being able to find a hit song is the reason that most people don't go any further in the business after they make their demo.

I believe that there are probably one or two hits or two great songs on every album. Other than that, most albums are a wash. That's one reason I think record sales have really dwindled in recent years. People want good songs and albums full of hit songs.

Record companies won't admit this, but they're probably not living in reality. When I was in college at Southern University, Alvin Batiste, the head of jazz studies, told me, "It's the little things at the crux of big institutions that cause their decline." I don't know if those are his own words or if he got them from somewhere, but they stuck with me. At a record company, the little things also happen to be the big things: the songs. Marketing, promotion, the hype and publicity, all come later. The very first ingredient—the song—is what's most important.

Finding great songs will be one of the biggest keys to your success before—and after—you make it big.

Hooking up with the players is hard to do

IF I AM A STAR PRODUCER/WRITER, LIKE Jimmy Jam, Terry Lewis, Timbaland or the Neptunes, I'm probably not going to give a hit song to an unknown artist who's making a demo. I'm most likely going to give it to one of my artists or the star I think will have the most success with the hits I think I've got.

Don't think for a minute that you're even going to get any of these guys on the phone now, if you can even find them. Let's be honest. If you're a nobody, Timbaland is not going to call you back.

It's the same with songwriters. An established songwriter who writes 100 or 200 songs a year is going to say, "I know what my four or five best songs are. So I'm going to hold out for the biggest record that I can put them on. If I go with Justin Timberlake or Mariah or some other high-profile artist, the record is going to sell a lot of copies, make me money and help me sustain my career for another couple of years." A primo songwriter or producer is going to say, "I'm not going to give this song—with all of its potential—to some new artist I don't know and who I don't trust yet, there's no way."

So you think it's just about you, but it's not. This is a mistake that labels, young A&R reps and young artists make. I'm speaking to you as an experienced producer and former senior VP of A&R. Yo, I'm telling you the God's honest truth. Most other people wouldn't tell you this.

So, guess what? You have a serious problem on your hands. At this stage in your career, when you're just starting out and have few if any contacts in the business, you have a one in a million chance of getting a hit song on your demo. So you're probably not going to get a record deal. You need the talent and you need a hit song.

If you *must* make a demo to land a record deal at this point, you still need to find a great songwriter. You need to do your homework to find out who the great songwriters are in your area. But you have to find out: Have they had any success of note? If they haven't, you need to move on to another one, because success is what you're after. Have they had any songs played on other people's records? Have those songs come out and have they been hits?

Finding a hit songwriter in your area might be tough unless you live in a big city where lots of hit songwriters tend to live, such as New York City, Los Angeles or Nashville. You might be able to find songwriters in your area, but they need to give you a hit, dude. The odds of that happening are low.

You could also try a music publisher. A music publisher

will give you a song, but probably won't give you a hit for the same reasons that the producer or songwriter won't.

This is what makes shows like *American Idol* so valuable. When you come on a show like *Idol*, you don't need a hit song. You just need to have "it." That's not easy either, but cuts out the step of having to have that hit song.

straight outta da Dawg's Mouth—*tip 14*

You watch TV—MTV, VH1, BET. You listen to the radio. You surf the Internet. Know what your competition is doing. You might say, "Yo. You're crazy. Madonna's not my competition!" Or "I don't care what Christina or 50 Cent are doing. I'm not competing against them."

Reality check: Yes, you are. Don't forget, you are ultimately trying to get on the same radio stations they're on. Sign with the same record labels. You have to be that good to make it.

So what should you do at this stage?

SO DUDE, NOW YOU CAN SEE WHY I'M saying that you're not really ready to make a recording demo yet. You don't know the business well enough. You don't know the players well enough.

If you persist in going ahead with trying to make this demo now, you could wind up in some kind of situation that you don't want to be in. I guarantee it. You could sign a bad management contract or a bad deal with a producer or songwriter and regret it for *years*.

You might want to have more experience and more knowledge about what you're doing before even attempting this gargantuan feat. Now you know why it's so hard to score a record deal. Having that combination of "it," a singular voice and a hit song is tough to come by. This is why few people get record deals. This is why not everyone's a star.

You don't know the players who can help you—and they don't know you. So now you have to start to educate yourself about the movers and shakers in the biz and start networking. I'm going to talk to you more about this in Chapter 7. But for now, scour the Internet and read every CD cover you can to find out who produces and writes songs for your favorite artists. Know who these people are because you will need them at some point, but it ain't now.

Try to meet people in the industry by going to songwriter meetings, seminars, concerts, parties, etc., in your area or elsewhere. Talk to other songwriters. Learn who the players are and try to get to know as many people as possible. It could take a long time to get to know even a few of the major players or people who are close to them. It will take tenacity and drive. You're going to use the same tools you used to find a teacher or a band. Just keep at it and it will happen for you.

Other ways in

THERE ARE OTHER WAYS TO GET YOURSELF STARTED in this business. You may not need to make a recording demo yet. If you're dope and you're great, guess what? You may get a background gig using your presentation demo. Or you might start singing on commercials. A songwriter might hear you sing, and say, "You know what? I want you to sing my song." Other people may hear you and want to help you. Remember, it's baby steps. Not trying to go for everything at once.

Using your presentation demo as a calling card, get out there and present your wares. Forget the recording demo for now and use that presentation demo to its fullest. Use it to help you to get work. Who knows, you may get a job singing backup for a big star like Britney Spears. Can you imagine the people that you'd meet then? Start to get your networking skills together now.

Other ways to make contacts

WHILE YOU'RE STILL GETTING IT TOGETHER, IT'S NOT a bad idea to have a job in a record store. You can hear records as soon as they come out, you'll get records at a discount and you'll be making a little bit of money. You'll be able to network with other musicians, singers and maybe even producers and other music makers who come into the store. You never know who you're going to meet. You're setting yourself up so that you're able to network.

You could work at a label as an intern or as an assistant or in the mailroom where many of today's A&R execs started. You'll be able to meet people and network this way. The thing to know about jobs in the industry is that you don't want to stay in them for too long.

Working at a label could give people the wrong impression of who you are—that you want to be a label employee and not a real artist. The record exec bigwigs may never see you as an artist now because you work for them. So for all of the networking you may do, you might be better working at 7-Eleven or Tower Records to earn money while you keep trying to get your career going.

Should you give stars like Courtney Love or Eminem your demo if you meet them?

LISTEN, MOST STARS DON'T WANT TO BE HAWKED. They're probably not going to stop and take a demo from you. You have to remember—stars are too liable at this point. They don't want to get sued. Too many people can claim that they handed a star a song and the star ripped it off.

So instead, find their producers, managers, songwriters or other people who work with them and see if you can hand it to them.

Even better, you need to meet people in the industry who could recommend you to an A&R rep at a label or to a producer. That's why this is going to be very difficult. That's why you need to network and meet as many people as you can.

That's why it's so important for you to prepare yourself as best you can and know beyond a shadow of a doubt that you're ready vocally or instrumentally. You should keep a presentation demo on you at all times in case you run into a legendary manager like Irving Azoff or a super-hot producer like Butch Vig. You never know. Try and put yourself in the right place at the right time if you can, to meet these people. This could all take a long time. I didn't know anybody in the beginning, but I networked and met people and got jobs that way.

Wherever you are in your development, college is always a good option. Always consider getting a full education. Your mom and dad probably told you to have something to fall back on. That's a good idea. I also highly recommend college because it gives you more time and more experience with professors and other professionals who can help you get yourself together and learn everything you can. I never heard of any artist who didn't make it because they knew too much.

So, come on, yo. Get your look right, get your groove on and keep it movin' . . .

Da Biz: The Who, What and Why

SO DAWG. YOU'RE ON YOUR WAY. MAYBE PROS you trust are telling you that you are ready to take on the world. You feel ready. You've polished your singing. Audiences at the clubs' you play really dig you. You've been networking like crazy and getting to know people in the business—and they're hopefully starting to hear your name and hear that you're someone really good.

You've reached the point where you may need to hire an attorney, a manager and possibly an agent. You may start working with songwriters or producers. Like most creative types, you probably don't want anything to do with contracts, spreadsheets or the fine print. You may think it's too boring or too scary to deal with. This chapter will outline the basics you need to know before you sign on the dotted line. Knowing what to expect will only help you get further in the business and free you up to become the best you can be.

Let the buyer beware

WHEN CHOOSING THE PROS YOU WANT TO WORK with or when dealing with anyone in the music business, you have to be careful. Know exactly who you're dealing with. Be alert all the time. Do your homework. Sponge and learn. The best way to protect yourself is to read everything you can—books, business journals and magazines such as *Billboard* and *Hits*—to understand the who, what and why. Talk to as many professionals as you can and ask them as many questions as possible. It's the only way to learn.

Every successful person in the music business has dealt with shady characters. Horror stories are legendary—managers stealing money. Producers signing wide-eyed newbies to lame deals. You are vulnerable, no matter where you are in your career, but especially when you're starting out. Some people you encounter may try and take you for everything you have because you're so green.

Keep in mind, yo, that you are going to make mistakes and may encounter people who will rip you off any chance they get. I can't tell you how many gigs I played where I was promised $50 or $60 and at the end of the night the bandleader would hand me $10 and say, "Sorry, man. It wasn't that sweet tonight." I'd ask, "Yo, man. Where's my money?" but he'd give me some sorry excuse like, "The club stiffed us. We didn't get all our money."

At this point, trust and believe almost no one. Remember, if it seems too good to be true, it probably is. That's why you also need a safety net—a good team made up of reputable people who will watch your back. That's why I'm talking to you about the business side of the industry right now.

You want to make sure that *all* the people who are working with you are above board, especially the people on your team. When looking for a lawyer, manager, etc., talk to other people and see who they recommend. It's usually best when someone you know and trust gives you a referral. Don't stop there. Check them out. Research their backgrounds. Make sure they're someone you can count on to help you go all the way.

First things first

YOU NEED TO START THINKING ABOUT FORMING YOUR team to help you through the music industry maze. This may mean hiring one or more of the following people: a lawyer, a manager, a producer, an agent and, later on in your career, an accountant and a business manager. You need this team to help you land a deal. Labels generally don't take unsolicited material. It has to come from a reputable attorney, manager, producer, etc. for the label to put its ears on it.

But what do you need to do first and in what order should this part of your journey take shape? I recommend finding a songwriter first to help you with your recording demo. You may also want to hook up with a music publisher to help you find songs for your demo. Then you'll need to find a producer. Then you'll need to get the business people involved—the lawyer, the manager and—down the road—an agent. In Chapter 7, I'll go more in-depth about how to power network with the A- and B-list players who can help you realize your dreams and get your groove on.

You don't have to hire these people on your team in this order, but this is what I recommend. This way, you're starting with the music and keeping that in the forefront at all times. My approach is very natural and makes music the centerpiece of your plan.

Working with a songwriter

AS I SAID IN CHAPTER 5, YOU'RE GOING to need at least one hit song on your recording demo. You're networking and are hopefully getting to know some pretty good songwriters. When trying to find the right one to work with you, you're asking: Do you write original songs? Could I use one on my demo?

The business of songwriting

IF YOU'RE TRYING YOUR HAND AT SONGWRITING, YOU may write songs alone or with someone. If you write songs with a partner, you have to determine what the splits are—who is going to own what percentage of the song if you record it or if someone else records it. This is how you make money as a songwriter. You get paid through the songwriting and publishing percentages you own. Agencies such as ASCAP, BMI and SESAC collect songwriter royalties for you and a publisher, if you have one.

A song's percentage is split into two parts—the songwriting and the publishing percentages. If you write a song alone, you own the song. You own 100 percent of the song-writing percentage and 100 percent of the publishing percentage.

If you write a song with a partner, the two of you would split it 50-50, assuming you each write half of the song.

Songs consist of three parts: the music (the beat, instrumentation and the chords), the melody and the lyrics. A typical pop song on the radio might be made up of an intro, a verse, a chorus, a second verse, the chorus again, a bridge and/or a B-verse and/or a middle-eight and/or a solo, and chorus out, meaning that the chorus will repeat itself until the song ends.

You could co-write all or parts of a song. Your percentage is always based upon what you and your co-writer or co-writers feel that your contribution was. You may have written the bridge while your partner wrote everything else, so you'll get a smaller percentage in this case.

Keep in mind that if you're working with a publisher, that company will get a percentage of the publishing part of the split.

Remember, always keep the splits clear with whoever you're working with. Get it straight up front, yo, so there are no problems down the road. You may also want to talk to your attorney about registering your songs so no one steals them.

My good friend Diane Warren is one of the most prolific song-writers on the planet. She has written more than one thousand of the world's most famous songs, including Celine Dion's "Because You Loved Me," Cher's "If I Could Turn Back Time," Toni Braxton's "Unbreak My Heart," LeAnn Rimes' and Trisha Yearwood's "How Do I Live," Belinda Carlisle's "I Get Weak," Christina Aguilera's "I Turn to You," *NSYNC's "That's When I'll Stop Loving You" and Kelly Clarkson's "Some Kind of Miracle." She has won tons of awards for her work and even has a star on the Hollywood Walk of Fame.

RANDY: Diane, hits are so hard to come by. But you've written hundreds. Where do you get your inspiration from?

DIANE: Everywhere. It sounds trite, but I get inspired all the time from everything. From things people say, or things I read or see. I'll be walking down the street and hear someone talking and a song title will come to me.

RANDY: What's your secret?

DIANE: For me, it's not a science. It's so magical. I can't explain the process. Somehow the ideas just come to me. I keep my antennae up and it just happens.

RANDY: How hard is it to write a hit song?

DIANE: There are a lot of ingredients that go into a song before it becomes a hit. The vocals have to be right. The production is important. And it has to be promoted to get on the radio.

Radio does a lot of research about what makes a song successful. Some records take longer to succeed than others. A lot of times radio stations will throw songs off the air if they don't get call-out, which is positive research. The reality is that some songs take longer for people to connect with and some of those may become huge hits. You have to fight a lot of battles for a song to make it.

RANDY: You're at the top of the top when it comes to songwriting. How hard is it for other people?

DIANE: It's very hard. But it's like anything that is hard. How difficult is it to have a hit movie if you've never had a hit movie before? You have to be good and work hard and have a little luck on your side.

RANDY: What advice do you have for songwriters who are on the way up?

DIANE: Just get good at your craft. Work hard. That's what worked for me. I have worked hard my whole life and still work as hard as I did at the beginning. I put my heart and soul and time into what I do. When I'm writing a song, it's all I think about. It's exhilarating. I love it.

RANDY: How important is a song on a demo or album?

DIANE: It all begins with the song. The music has to be good. If you are a band or an artist, your music had better be good or else all the other stuff doesn't matter. Nobody's going to sign you if you don't have good songs.

RANDY: How good does your demo have to be to get a record deal?

DIANE: The song must be a hit, however you produce the demo. If you are sending out demos, send your best three songs. If you've written the songs, make sure that the song is right for the artist. Don't send a rock song to an R&B artist just because you think the song is great. Casting is very important to get songs placed with artists.

RANDY: If you are a singer and you need hit songs to help you get a record deal, how do you recommend going about finding good songs?

DIANE: If I were a singer, I would try to get important people excited about me. I would try to get a great manager or lawyer on my team.

If a top manager called me about someone new, I would be more likely to see that person. Or maybe I might hear something and want to work with that artist. Who knows?

But it is very hard to get a hit songwriter to give you a song if you are just starting out. I probably wouldn't unless I have a vested interest in a new artist. If they don't have a deal, I probably wouldn't give them a song unless I was blown away, and that's rare. If someone doesn't have a deal, I don't want them shopping for a deal with a brand-new song I just wrote.

You have to find clever ways of getting yourself heard by the right people. You have to go through every angle. You've got to network and you've got to be in a music center such as Los Angeles, New York or Nashville. Get to know everybody.

Play some clubs. Get a buzz going. A grass-roots kind of thing. Build a following so people can get interested in you.

RANDY: What advice do you have for singers?

DIANE: My advice is to always use the best song you can, whether you write it or someone else writes it. I think that holds a lot of artists back right now. Often, an artist's first album will have a bunch of hits they didn't write. Then when their next album comes around, they say, "We have to write because it gives us credibility." But if you write a bunch of lame songs, the album's not going to sell.

So I say to singers, use the best songs you can on your demo or album. Search them out. If you write some, write some, but use the best ones. And if you don't write them, it doesn't really matter. The audience is going to think you wrote them anyway. People think Steven Tyler wrote "I Don't Want to Miss a Thing" even though I wrote the song.

RANDY: What mistakes do beginning songwriters often make?

DIANE: Putting all of their energy into one song.

RANDY: What makes a hit song?

DIANE: It's something that touches you. Something you can feel and that moves you on some level. It's just a combination of great music and great lyrics that were born to be together.

The music publisher

LET'S SAY YOU'RE A SINGER AND YOU CAN'T find hit songs for your recording demo anywhere. None of the songwriters in your area have anything worth recording. You've gotten to know some C-list songwriters in New York City, but none of them have a song that will rock the charts. At this point, you could go to a music publishing company, which can help you find the songs you need. Keep in mind that this doesn't necessarily mean that they're going to be hit songs.

If you're a singer and a prolific writer, you definitely want a publisher to help you out. If they love you as an artist and, more important, as an aspiring songwriter, they may sign you to a publishing deal, finance your demo and help you land a record deal. One thing to know: A publisher doesn't get paid until the song is used, say, on a record, in a TV commercial or in a movie.

Publishing deals are as hard to get as record deals are. Publishers don't just sign anybody up. If you do sign with a publisher, you may get some sort of an advance. But the publisher won't get paid until the song starts getting played, i.e., making money. They get paid by taking a piece of the publishing percentage.

One of my big Dawgs, Kenny MacPherson, is the president of Chrysalis Music Group USA, one of the biggest music publishers around. He's a 30-year veteran of the music industry and has worked in music publishing for 15 years. He has worked with artists such as Radiohead, Outkast, Savage Garden, Soul Asylum, Green Day and Supertramp, to name a few.

RANDY: So Kenny, what is music publishing?

KENNY: Music publishing is a very creative and very exciting part of the business. The role of the music publisher is very broad, but basically, a music publisher is there to support the songwriter's creative endeavors. A very proactive music publisher can enhance a songwriter's career at different stages, and can perform various roles, including giving management, legal and business advice. A music publisher does not take the place of these people, but is there to supplement their efforts and be a team player.

A music publisher's role includes, but is not limited to, (1) copyrighting and protecting a writer's musical compositions worldwide; (2) properly registering the songs with the agencies and societies that help collect the royalties from the sale and performance of the songs (e.g., the Harry Fox Agency, ASCAP, BMI and SESAC); and (3) promoting the songs to all areas of the entertainment industry.

RANDY: If I'm just starting out, do you recommend going to a music publisher?

KENNY: The great thing for songwriters and artists is that they have choices. If you fully understand the role of a music publisher, then seeking one out in the very beginning can be helpful. A music publisher can guide you in your songwriting. A music publisher can introduce you to other writers, producers, lawyers, agents and record company personnel.

All publishing companies help promote their talent's works. Some music publishers are proactive and help develop talent, such as Chrysalis Music. There are others that just administer copyrights.

Performing rights societies like ASCAP and BMI are a good place for writers to go when they're starting out. They can provide guidance and help introduce beginning songwriters to the business.

RANDY: Are music publishers the only companies that deal with publishing?

KENNY: Quite often, law firms handle publishing and the administration of a writer's work. But they usually don't have any professional creative managers to help promote the writer's works.

RANDY: If I'm a singer but not a songwriter, can I work with a music publisher?

KENNY: If you're a singer only, you could approach a music publisher to try and see if they have songs to help you get a record deal. All music publishing companies have staff writers—people who are not recording artists but who write songs for other people. If you are a singer and you wanted to

sing other people's songs, you could contact a music publisher, who may be able to help find the right songs for your
style of music.

RANDY: Can you use these songs on your recording demo?

KENNY: Music publishing houses are definitely a place to go
to find a song for your demo. They all have hit songwriters
working with them.

RANDY: Do you have to pay for a song to use on your demo?

KENNY: No, you don't. Basically, it's about getting in touch
with somebody at the publishing company, explaining what
you're trying to do. If the publisher agrees to work with you,
you can record a song of theirs in demo form to present to
record companies to see if they're interested in signing you.
If you make a record and you use that song, then the publishing company is paid by the sale and performance of that
record.

RANDY: Can a publisher help you to get a record deal?

KENNY: Absolutely. If you're a songwriter and a music publisher hears your songs and believes in you, they can then
help develop you, work with you and help make the presentation to the record company.

If you're a singer but not a songwriter and you meet a
music publisher and they think you have a great voice, they
can help you develop by giving you great songs to then
present to the record companies.

RANDY: Where are music publishers located?

KENNY: Most are in New York City, Nashville and Los Angeles. There are other good publishers scattered around the country.

RANDY: How do you suggest approaching a music publisher?

KENNY: You can approach a music publisher cold by sending in a sample of your work. This is known as unsolicited material, which means you are trying to get in the door without knowing anybody. Because we live in a litigious society, a lot of record and music publishing companies are loath to take unsolicited material.

You'll have better luck if you've been introduced by somebody from a performing rights society, a lawyer or a manager—or anyone who has a contact there. One time a guy working on my house said, "My nephew is a singer." You hear this all the time, but he turned out to be great. You never know when and how you're going to hear about new people with talent. In the music business, you have to be open to the unexpected.

RANDY: How should you send material to a publisher?

KENNY: You need to learn how to present your material in the correct way. Some people will send material in without a name or return address. Do you think we're mind readers? You have to include your name, address, phone number and e-mail address, if you have one, so the person you're sending it to has some way of getting back to you.

You always have to be professional. You have to be prepared to work really hard. You have to care passionately about what you do. You have to understand the fine line between being a pest and being persistent. Don't call the company 10 times a day to see if somebody got your tape or CD and what's happening with it.

You have to be realistic. If you send music or songs to companies and you don't hear back within a month, you're probably not going to hear back. You have to understand there is so much music and so many people out there trying to break into the business as well. It's highly competitive.

RANDY: Any other words of wisdom?

KENNY: The music business is tough, but people shouldn't be disheartened. A lot of people, who want to be artists but can't make it in that field, should not give up hope of working in the industry and should look for other areas to work in if they have a belief in and passion for music. I have people working for me who were musicians in bands that didn't make it, but who have become publishing executives. I know people in all areas of the industry who tried to be artists and did not make it, but have gone on to be highly successful in the music business.

Don't give up on your dream—just be prepared to alter it if necessary.

Going the singer/songwriter route

BEING A SONGWRITER COULD BE A BIG PLUS for your career as a singer or musician. Mariah Carey is an amazing songwriter. Of her 15 number-one hits, she co-wrote 14. (Her fifteenth number-one song was the Jackson Five's "I'll Be There.")

straight outta da **Expert's Mouth**

My good friend Judy Stakee, VP of A&R at Warner Chappell Music in Los Angeles, has worked with stars from Jewel to Michelle Branch.

RANDY: So Judy, how did Sheryl Crow work with your company to get her solo career going?

JUDY: She was a fabulous singer/songwriter who was trying to get herself a record deal. She was already a great backup singer with perfect pitch who could play most any instrument. But she still had to figure out how she was going to differentiate herself and figure out how to go from being a backup singer to being a star. When you're a backup singer, you are a chameleon. Singing backup for Don Henley is completely different from singing backup for Michael Jackson.

As a publisher, you work with artist/writers who are trying to establish themselves. So when we met, we worked on defining who she was through her own material and sound. We've done this with many artists. Sheryl and I would sit and she would play me her songs, looking for feedback. So I acted as an editor.

Publishers wear many hats. We're agents, managers, teachers, psychologists and babysitters. We help you pre-

Hooking up with a music publisher helped Sheryl Crow launch her career. She had been singing backup for Michael Jackson, Don Henley, the late George Harrison and other big names. But she was trying to get her own record deal. So she worked with Judy Stakee at Warner Chappell Music in Los Angeles to help get her solo career off the ground.

pare for meetings with A&R people. I even took country singer Kellie Coffey shopping so she'd look great for her record company meetings.

As a publisher, we give you time to develop, market yourself and experiment. Most record companies don't have the time anymore to develop acts. We help in that development—anything from financing demos, arranging for musicians and a studio for a demo to fixing you up with other co-writers so your material is the best. We set up meetings with managers, lawyers and agents. A publisher is vital to the career of a songwriter. We work with your record company and the rest of your team.

If you do not have a record deal and work with a publisher, you still have a family to go to where you can be creative and develop.

RANDY: How hard is it to land a publishing deal?

JUDY: It is difficult to land a publishing deal. But if you're good, it can be the easiest thing in the world. Be prepared. When you meet with publishers, don't give them 20 songs. Give them the three best songs you've written. And do your homework.

The producer

IF YOU'VE HOOKED UP WITH A PRIMO SONGWRITER or pub-lisher and think you have a great song, now you may be ready to make a recording demo. If so, now's the time to hire a producer. A producer orchestrates everything to do with recording your demo or, later on, that album you may be working on. The producer finds the studio for you and hires the people to help you make the demo, such as the mixer, the engineer, the programmer, background singers and musicians.

You find a producer the same way you found your teacher, the band you play with and your songwriter, if you have one. Talking to people. Getting recommendations. Asking pros you trust.

This is where family connections or friends can be helpful. Your third cousin may know Fred Durst's manager, who may know of a great producer for you—and who might even be able to get your demo to a label when you're done.

At this point, the producer may want to sign you to a production deal, sign you to his own label or get you to pay for the cost of these demos. The producer may say, "I need you to pay me $3,000 or $5,000 a song—or more—for my services. And you have to pay all my musicians."

So here is where the money you've earned at your gigs and at your day job hits the road. This is when you may want to hire an attorney to help you navigate any deals. Remember, up to this point, you haven't signed anything with anyone and you still don't really want to sign anything with anyone if you can help it, but you're considering it.

Production deals—the pros and cons

WHEN PEOPLE ARE JUST GETTING STARTED, PRODUCERS OFTEN offer them deals that sound good. But you have to be extra careful to make sure the deal is a good one for you. A production deal means that you sign a contract with a producer or production company. That company will usually take care of costs like making your demo. But if you land a record deal, you will have to pay the production company a percentage of what you get. With all the other costs you're going to have—attorney's fees, management fees, etc.—that could add up.

Signing a production deal doesn't guarantee that you'll end up with a record deal, either. A production company is going to shop your demo around just as you would.

The pluses are that a production company has more experience and probably more contacts than you do at this point. And if you're lucky enough to have a super-hot producer discover you, he or she could open major doors for you in the industry.

But a bad production deal could lock you up for a long time. That's why you need a lawyer to read the contract and make sure you're not signing your life away. It's always best to sign up for the shortest term possible. You and your lawyer have to figure out what's best for you.

When people are coming at you hard, wanting to charge you all kinds of money, it's a sign that something is not right with this situation. Always check with your lawyer to make sure you're not going to get hurt.

You don't always have to sign a production deal. A producer may work for you "on spec"—on speculation—which means he'll get paid later if things work out for you. This is where you have to be careful and where having an attorney to guide you is a good idea.

A producer may also hear you sing and say, "Yo! That's hot! I want to be a part of that." The producer may want to work with you for free. You may not be asked to sign a production deal. The producer knows you are destined for something big and wants to be a part of it.

But the producer may want some kind of a guarantee that if you use these songs he produces for you, you will let him produce them on the record—if you get a deal. The producer is saying that he wants to remain attached to this project. This is an option that you may want to pursue. Always run it by your lawyer first.

straight outta da Expert's Mouth

Jimmy Jam and Terry Lewis are one of the most successful producing teams in the history of the business. These two songwriter/producers—my boys—are truly legendary. They have been joined musically at the hip for more than 30 years and have worked with superstars, including Beyoncé, Janet Jackson, Sting, Michael Jackson, Usher, Mary J. Blige, Mariah Carey, Patti LaBelle, Mya, the Isley Brothers, Shaggy, Kelly Price, Boyz II Men, New Edition and Rod Stewart, among many, many others.

Jam and Lewis have worked on more than 100 albums that have gone gold, platinum or multi-platinum. They have produced 16 number-one pop hits, making them the number-two pop producers of all time, according to *Billboard*, and have scooped up numerous Grammy Awards. These Dawgs are truly brilliant.

Jimmy is going to share a little of his wisdom with you.

RANDY: So Jimmy, what does a producer do?

JIMMY: A producer is like a director on a movie set. A director's job is to get the best performance out of the actor. Sometimes the director on a movie set may say, "Deliver the line this way," or "Let's change that line. You don't sound natural saying that line. So let's do this instead."

A producer makes the same types of decisions when working on a song or an album. A producer tries to get the best performance out of an artist. A producer does whatever is necessary to make that happen. A producer sometimes has to be a psychologist, sometimes a cook, sometimes a masseuse. You have to treat everybody differently to motivate them. You have to become a confidant. You want somebody to be very open with you.

You have to be open with them, since the relationship is also based on criticism. You are telling them, "You are singing flat. You are singing sharp. You are in front of the beat."

The relationship between artists and producers becomes very intimate because you spend a lot of time together. In trying to figure out how to get the best performance out of an artist, you realize that some people need to be encouraged a lot. Even if they don't sound good, you have to continually tell them that they sound great because they don't respond well to criticism. Other people want you to be brutally honest with them.

One of the things that Terry and I have always prided ourselves on is getting the best vocal performance out of someone. That involves pushing the right buttons to get the right performance.

As a producer, figuring out how somebody likes to work can help to get the best performance out of them. Some people like to work during the day. Some people like to work at night. Some people like to get to the studio, walk right in and start singing right away. Some people like to get to the studio, maybe have a bite to eat, maybe play a game of pool or relax.

For instance, we're in the studio now with New Edition. The first record we did with them was the *Heart Break* album in 1988, so we go back quite a while. Ralph Tresvant, who's in the group, just wants to walk in and sing. So you have everything ready to go. The mike is already on. You've already got the song ready.

He will stay in there until you practically kick him out. You have to kick him out because he won't ever leave. He won't tell you, "My voice is tired." You, as the producer, have to listen for that. That's the way he works and you obviously get a great result out of it.

If you tell another member of the group, Johnny Gill, "Let's work at six o'clock," Johnny will show up at six o'clock. He will be relatively on time. But he'll say, "Has everybody eaten? Where's the menu?" He'll make a few phone calls. Get on the Internet. Whatever. As a producer, what I know is if Johnny gets there at six o'clock, I need to be ready for him to sing at eight o'clock, which means there are two hours that I can do other things that I need to do.

An executive producer usually oversees the entire album,

including song selection and those types of things, particularly in hip-hop and R&B. That can also be an A&R person's job. A producer deals more with just the individual songs. The producer usually works on a song-by-song basis.

A producer's decisions can be technical, like choosing the type of microphone you use or whether you're going to use analog or digital recording. A producer can be involved in the arrangement of a song, deciding which musicians or programmers to hire. At the end of the day, a producer can also determine whether the artist's performance in the studio was good or not and whether you want to go back and do it again.

As a producer, you have to have a good set of ears and a good set of instincts about what sounds pleasing. It's good if a producer is a fan. The way Terry and I pick the artists that we work with has a lot to do with whether we're fans of the artist. If we're fans of the artist, then it's really easy for us, from a fan's perspective, to know whether what the artist is doing is going to be pleasing. We ask ourselves, if we're going to spend $10 on a CD, what would we like to hear on that CD as fans of this artist?

If we're not fans of that artist or we don't feel inspired by someone, we won't work with them, no matter how popular they are. As a producer, if you don't feel that creative spark with somebody where you want to put in the long hours and you really want to put the time into it, then you shouldn't work with that person.

A big part of it is you have to love what you do. I'm a big fan of music. Always have been. It's in my blood. Whenever I used to hear songs on the radio when I was young, in the back of my mind I always said, "I could produce that." And not only did I feel I could do it, but I thought I could do it better. That's part of what drove me to do it. When I got into it, it was really tough. But you just use your instincts that a casual listener would use, but you delve deeper into it. It's one thing to say, 'That sounds good." That's part of it, but the other part is how to actually make it sound good.

As a producer, you never stop learning. Technology changes. New artists come with new ideas and you have to be receptive to them. You can't ever get stuck on the whole notion of "what used to be" was better. You can get so stuck on the way things were done in the past that you don't look at what the new things are and that's very, very dangerous. We've seen a lot of people do that. That's one of the things that we've never done. You have to be open to new ideas. I think being accepting of new things has been part of our longevity.

RANDY: What can a producer help you with if you are just starting out?

JIMMY: The line is a little more blurred now because there are so many opportunities to record at home. The producer in the old days really was the guy with the money who financed everything.

That slowly segued into people producing in the more traditional sense to get the best performance out of the artist. A songwriter would bring a song in. The producer would produce it. Everybody had their role. You would go to a big studio to record and you would need all those people to get it done.

Nowadays, you can record on your laptop and do almost as good a job as you could in a professional studio. You don't even have to have an actual keyboard with sounds in it. You can download the sounds off the Internet. You can do your vocals in the same way. So now you've become a producer and songwriter, if you've written the song, as well as the musician and programmer.

What a producer brings at any level is objectivity. Even if you're doing everything yourself, to have an educated ear listening to what you are doing is a good thing. Someone to say to you, "Hey, I think you can sing this better."

RANDY: How do you recommend finding a producer?

JIMMY: I'm a big fan of networking. I think probably in any city in the country, there are people who have equipment and do tracks. When I'm lecturing for various programs, I'll ask people, "How many people are songwriters?" and people will raise their hands. I'll ask, "How many people are singers?" Then I'll say, "Now everybody look at each other because you're all going to need each other." There's always a singer who just sings and doesn't write but needs songs. There's a songwriter who doesn't sing but needs a singer. Or a producer who is looking to work with somebody. These people exist right under your nose.

The person who is a good producer for you is a person you probably get along with and feel a connection with. It's not a right or wrong thing. You certainly don't want anybody who shoves a big contract in your face and says, "Sign all this stuff and I'll produce your demo."

RANDY: Speaking of bad deals, how do you know when a production deal is good or one you should stay away from?

JIMMY: You try to find a lawyer that you trust. Once again, a lot of this stuff is common sense. There's no cut and dried way to know. Use your instincts. If it sounds too good to be true, then it probably is too good to be true. If somebody feeds you a line saying, "I'm going to do all this for you. You don't have to do anything for me," that's when a red flag should go up.

A lot of times it is a tradeoff. Somebody has talent and there's somebody else who has money and no talent and is willing to put some backing behind you to do it. You just try to pick people you trust and who you feel comfortable with. This is very subjective. There is no Good Housekeeping seal of approval for producers.

Word of mouth is always a good thing. Talk to people you know. Look things up on the Internet. Go to allmusic.com and see if somebody's credentials actually line up. If a producer says they have worked with a certain person, then their name should show up as a writer or producer on those projects. If it doesn't, then that would be a red flag to you.

RANDY: How do you get top producers to notice you if you're just starting out?

JIMMY: Everybody does it in a different way. We have a website—flytetyme.com, which has information on it about demo tips: what to send, how to send it, who to send it to. We include an address where you can send demos to us.

We look for star quality. It's one of those things where

somebody either has it or they don't have it. They may have star quality because they sing really well or look really good or dance really well. If they have a combination of all those things, boy, wouldn't that be great.

If you see them on video or hear them on a demo, you look to see, do they light up the room? Do they have an energy about them? Do they have something that you want to share with somebody? The thing I always go by is if I see somebody or hear somebody and I immediately want to call Terry and say, "Oh my God. You gotta hear this," or "Oh my God. You gotta see this." For me, it's something that makes me excited.

RANDY: What advice do you have for people who are just starting out?

JIMMY: My number-one piece of advice is like the Boy Scouts' motto—be prepared. Preparation is so much of it. You never know where your break is going to come from. I can't guarantee whether it's going to happen or not happen, but I can guarantee that when that break does happen, you had better be prepared.

If you're a singer, you are singing every day. You are listening to singers. You are trying to take vocal lessons and doing vocal exercises.

Everybody needs to prepare differently. If I want to become a producer, I would look up every record that my favorite producer did. I'd look up Timbaland or Dr. Dre or Jam & Lewis on the Internet. Those types of things.

You should do all this naturally, by the way, if you love what you're doing. You should have a burning desire to do this. Terry and I gave up everything to make music. We sacrificed family. Credit. We were broke. Terry sold a car so we could buy a four-track tape recorder and a microphone and a keyboard so we could produce our demos. We stayed in a 10-foot-by-10-foot room with two cots in it. We ate one meal a day. Walked everywhere. But we weren't thinking, "We're really sacrificing." We were gladly doing it. We were loving it.

Everybody was looking at us, going, "Oh, man. Y'all are messing up. Y'all are out there starving in LA." We were like, "Yeah, whatever. We're not starving out here." We were so into it. And when we got our break early on from a trio of music industry legends—Leon Sylvers III, Clarence Avant and Dick Griffey—we were ready. Producer Leon Sylvers told us, "I like the demo you produced on the little four-track in your apartment. Go into a real studio and go do these songs."

We literally slept in the studio. We didn't even go home, we were so happy to be in the studio. We didn't leave. He said, "Do one song. It will probably take you a couple of days." We said, "Hey. We did five songs in two days." He was like, "What?"

Then Dick Griffey, the founder and head of the Solar label, said, "I have this group called Climax and I want you to produce a song for them." He said, "You can't do it with the budget that you have." And we said, "Yeah, watch it. We can."

Tabu Records founder Clarence Avant said, "I want you guys to do a couple songs for SOS band," which turned out to be our big break and our first number-one record.

It was all because we were ready. It was all about preparing. When we actually got in the studio to make music, that was the dream. We were like, "Oh my God. We're in the studio. We're never leaving." And we haven't left since. We have our own studios now.

Other advice I have? Get to know the industry that you want to become a part of. You should be reading the trades every week—*Billboard, Hits* and *R&R,* etc.

Know the players. I always read the liner notes of the albums when I was growing up because I was always interested in who did what. I can't tell people to do that enough. A lot of times you're at the point where you get your demo done and you have your package together and you say, "Who do I send it to?" Most of that information is out there. It's all out there for you.

A lot of people say that they're waiting for their break. And I tell them let's substitute the word "preparing" for the word "waiting." That is what you should be doing. You shouldn't be waiting for anything to happen. You should be preparing for when it does happen.

To me, the more people you send your demo to, the better, because it increases your odds of somebody hearing it.

Get used to rejection. There's going to be a lot of rejection. Maybe 99 people telling you no, but you've got to go for that 100th person, which could be the yes. A lot of people get disappointed and spend too much energy with a chip on their shoulder. Then you're spending too much energy on negativity. It affects the way you go about doing your business and the way you deal with people.

In the spotlight

IF YOU THINK IT'S UNLIKELY THAT A PRODUCER or manager or someone else in the biz is going to discover you, think again. You never know who's going to hear you or who you're going to meet.

In August, my wife, Erika, and I were at Caesar's Palace in Las Vegas, where Mariah Carey was performing. This was her first show in the States after touring in South Korea and Japan. As the tour's musical director, I was trying to tune the show up for its run in the U.S. We were walking through the Caesar's Palace Forum shops when a 15-year-old girl who was with her mom stopped me. As I've said, I don't mind when people come up to me because I never know where I'm going to find great talent. People say I'm a cool, nice guy, so maybe that's why I seem so approachable. The girl said, "I'm too young to try out for *Idol*. But I'm a really good singer. I think I can really do it." So I said, "Prove it."

So she sang for me in the middle of the mall. Yo, it was crazy busy in there. People everywhere. I put people on the spot like this because I want to see if they are bold enough to prove right there and then that they have it. If their voices stand up, we might actually be doing some talking.

She was really good. She had a great look. She had an old soul vibe goin' on. And she had her head together. I told her I would stay in touch with her. So she's on my radar now. So once in a while, that's how it happens. When you get your shot, you have to be ready.

Yo, you want to make sure that the people on your team are not in cahoots with any of the other people you're working with. That they're not taking advantage of you. If you live in a small area where there's only one good entertainment lawyer and your producer has the same lawyer, find another lawyer. Don't use a manager if that manager works with the attorney. You always want to work with someone who has objectivity and is only looking out for you.

Finding an attorney

A GOOD ATTORNEY IS GOING TO BE ONE of the most important members of your team. You want to make sure to work with an entertainment or music industry lawyer. You don't want to hire your cousin's divorce lawyer or your dad's insurance attorney. You want to work with someone who is familiar with the ins and outs of this crazy business.

Once again, you'll go about finding an attorney just like you found the teacher, songwriter, etc. Do your homework. Do your research. Ask around. You should have these skills down by now. Remember, you have to be resourceful to get what you need.

You want to find the best attorney you can afford. You want this person to tell you which way to go. He or she can answer questions like: Is the producer I like reputable? Should I sign this contract? The attorney should watch your back for you. The attorney may also have connections that can really help you.

straight outta da *Expert's Mouth*

LA-based entertainment attorney L. Lee Phillips is a partner at Manatt, Phelps and Phillips. My buddy Lee is one of the best in the business and reps superstars from Barbra Streisand and the Eagles to Lisa Marie Presley and Tracy Chapman.

RANDY: So Lee, what does an entertainment attorney do?

LEE: Entertainment attorneys are responsible for a wide range of things. In the music business, an entertainment attorney can represent artists or companies. Since so many artists start early—16, 17 or 18 or even younger—entertainment lawyers tend to have young clients who seek advice from a business or legal standpoint.

When you're just starting out, an entertainment attorney will tell you how the whole business works and what kind of contracts you should expect to enter into. Your lawyer will help you deal with personal managers, agents, business managers, accountants and publicists.

Lawyers in the music business usually act as business advisers as well. They can help you decide if a deal is good or not, advise you of pitfalls you should be concerned about, what kind of rights you should have if you are a performing artist who writes your own material, and what it means to own your own publishing and copyrights.

A top entertainment lawyer knows a lot of people in the business and can make phone calls and introductions to executives at record companies, agents, personal managers or accountants.

If an artist seems to be very talented, a lawyer might shop you around—send your CD around to record companies and producers to try to place you. My firm tends not to do that, but on occasion we try to introduce artists to people who might be interested in signing them to a deal.

Entertainment attorneys also work with established artists. They already know the business and have contracts, so they look to us to improve their contracts, advise them on how to get out of contracts and make new deals for them, which we do from a legal and business standpoint.

Many artists like Barbra Streisand are involved in more than just music. So you often end up advising these kinds of clients on things that are unrelated to the music side, such as TV or movies.

Since your clients are individuals and not corporations, but are involved in many different things, you usually act as general counsel for them. You can help them with everything from real estate matters to tax, litigation, and protection of privacy, especially if you work for a large firm. Other attorneys in the firm who are expert in these areas would handle these types of matters.

RANDY: How do clients usually find you?

LEE: Someone usually refers an artist to me. Sometimes other artists or business and personal managers make the referrals. Oftentimes, it is simply by reputation.

RANDY: How will an attorney protect you?

LEE: An attorney will protect you in contract negotiations. The lawyer will try to get you the shortest contract in terms of length of time for the greatest amount of money and royalties. When making a deal with a record company, the lawyer will try and reserve as many rights as possible for you. The lawyer will make sure you do not give away merchandising or publishing rights. It is important that the contract protects you.

If you write your own material, the lawyer can protect you by making sure the material is copyrighted.

A lawyer will also help you when you sign an agency agreement. The lawyer should make sure you're working with the right agency. The lawyer will try to get the best agency agreement for you, for the shortest period and the right percentage.

RANDY: What won't a lawyer do for me?

LEE: Many people starting out think that lawyers handle their money, but they do not. A lawyer should not invest your money for you.

Most lawyers will not shop you around to various companies. They may make calls to contacts they know on your behalf, but will not try to place you.

Most will not act as your agent for personal appearances. They will not file tax returns for you, either. That is for the accountant to do.

They usually do not act as personal managers, though a personal manager sometimes does the same thing as a lawyer. That is why we have to work together sometimes.

Lawyers usually will not be involved on the creative side of things. They leave that to the personal manager. A lawyer should not tell a client what songs to sing, what producers, managers or musicians to hire, what rhythm to use or what key to sing in, etc.

RANDY: What should people look for when hiring a lawyer?

LEE: You want to hire someone who has a great deal of experience in the business, representing talent primarily. I represent companies too, but I am known primarily for representing talent. But you also want a lawyer who has seen both sides of the issue—the talent and the record company—so they understand the big picture.

You want to work with a lawyer who knows a lot of people in the business, who did well in law school, who is well-respected and who seems to be interested in what you are doing.

RANDY: What should you look for when you are signing a contract with a manager, agent or record company?

LEE: When signing a contract with a personal manager, normally you pay a manager 15 or 20 percent of your earnings. It should not be more than 20 percent. You want to know how that percentage is computed. That is where you need a lawyer to advise you.

When you hire a personal manager, you hire someone who is going to work non-exclusively for you. It is somewhat one-sided. The manager can represent 50 other artists, but you cannot hire another manager. So you should be very careful about how long the contract is for, because if you sign something for five years, say, and you think the manager is not doing a good job, you may be obligated to pay him or her for a long period of time. You want as short-term a contract as you can get, whether it is one and a half or two years, so that if you do not like the manager, you can get out of the relationship sooner than not.

Contracts with agents are pretty standard. If you are a member of a union, you are already protected because the union has negotiated the contract.

When signing a record contract, there are many things to look for, but here are the main points: What is the advance? How much money are they committed to pay me? How long is the term and how much am I committed to the record company? When you are dealing with record companies, you usually measure this in albums. So a contract may be for one album plus six options for six more.

That means that they will give you, say, $250,000 for the first album, including recording costs. If the album does well, the record company then has an option to do another one, which you are obligated to do.

You also want to know, what royalty rate am I going to get? Artists are paid a royalty rate for each record sold and that is really how they make their money. This is where you need a lawyer to tell you whether this is a good or bad rate.

You also want to pay attention to the point structure—the royalty. Fifteen points usually means you are getting 15 percent of the retail price of the album with deductions. But this varies from company to company and it is changing. For years, it used to mean 15 percent of the suggested retail price with deductions. It is now changing to what is called the price per dealer, or PPD, which is a wholesale price. So you may get a higher number of points on a wholesale price, which is lower than the retail price. So in some cases, a deal for 25 points may be worth less than one for 15 points.

The next thing you want to look for is how much creative control the contract gives you. You would like to have as many creative controls and approvals and involvement as you can get. You want to approve what songs you are singing, what producer is hired and which studio is used. The record company wants you to have as few approvals as possible. So there is always give and take on both sides. The creative side is very important to an artist, and it may be a major difference as to whether an artist wants to be with a particular company.

RANDY: What does it cost to hire a lawyer to sign a record deal?

LEE: A lot of lawyers charge 5 percent of the gross earnings. We usually charge a reasonable fee based primarily on an hourly rate, but we try to tie the fee into the deal. We try to accommodate younger artists as best we can so we can be with them for the long run. We hope that the artist will have a long career.

A new artist deal can range from $7,500 in fees for a simple new artist deal to maybe $25,000 or more, if there is a bidding war for the artist, for instance.

Finding a manager

A MUSIC MANAGER HELPS YOU OVERSEE EVERY ASPECT of your career—including organizing your schedule, keeping on top of your legal and financial affairs, promoting you within the industry, advising you on deals, negotiating with record companies and just being there to lean on when things get crazy. If you have a good manager you trust, he or she can help you figure out who's on your side and who's not.

A lot of times, artists don't hire a manager until after their careers really take off. Keep in mind that you could hire a manager before the attorney, if you find a good one. But you'll still need to have a lawyer review the contract with a manager before you sign on the dotted line.

straight outta da Expert's Mouth

One of the best managers in the known world is my true friend Johnny Wright. He is the man who helped make artists like *NSYNC, Justin Timberlake, Britney Spears and the Backstreet Boys multi-platinum stars. He's got that magic touch.

RANDY: So Johnny, what does a manager do?

JOHNNY: A manager is like a traffic cop. A manager's responsibility is to take everyone and move them from place to place without causing congestion.

A manager will make sure that the band gets to

rehearsals. That the tour manager has the proper information to get the band from the hotel to the rehearsal. That whatever vision the artist has musically for the band to perform is relayed to the musical director. That the buses and the hotel and everything that it takes to move an artist from place to place is coordinated.

The manager makes sure that marketing and promotion at the label understand the wishes of the artist so that by the time that record comes out, everything is in place and the audience will know that the record is coming and is in stores. The manager coordinates MTV appearances, studio time and producers and writers who are going to help create the record. The manager coordinates photographers, and hair and makeup people and locations and makes sure pictures for the album and publicity are done.

So again, the manager is responsible for the movement of the artist from A to Z and for making sure that everything from the most minute situation, including what color shoes and socks an artist should wear depending on the artist's preference, is taken care of so all that artist has to do is show up and be creative.

RANDY: Why do you need a manager if you're just starting out?

JOHNNY: A manager is the voice of the artist. A manager is someone who should have relationships in the music business to help establish whatever an artist might need, whether it's hiring a writer or producer or getting into a recording studio. Once that package is finished, he or she has to be the person who goes to the record company and allows the record company to see the artist and hear the music and coordinate the signing of the deal. This is the person who will set up meetings with PR people and attorneys.

In essence, a manager is someone who must have knowledge of everything the artist needs to do. There are many people out there who are great singers who are never going to get heard because they don't have a way to get to the people who make the deals. So a good manager should be someone who is connected.

RANDY: How do you find a manager?

JOHNNY: You have to do research and find artists whose careers have followed the path that you want to follow. Find out who that manager is and do everything under the sun that you can to try to get that manager to hear you, whether it's camping outside their doorstep or going to their favorite restaurant.

There are a million ways people get demo tapes to me or find me. If a manager is a good manager and they're always on the lookout for new talent, they will understand the difference between someone who is hungry and dedicated and someone who's a nutcase.

RANDY: How do you recommend approaching a potential manager?

JOHNNY: How you approach someone is important. If you do your research, you will find out what the manager likes and start a conversation with that. For example, if someone knows that maybe I'm a guy who likes the Boston Red Sox, you could start off by saying, "Hey, what do you think about the Boston Red Sox?" You get into a conversation, and from that you can always work your way, very subtly, into, "I'm a singer. If you have some time and if you're looking for someone, you should give me a shot. I'm very dedicated and willing to work hard. Here is my phone number."

RANDY: When do you recommend getting a manager?

JOHNNY: There are some managers out there who won't touch an artist until they've already produced a demo. There are some managers out there who won't even get involved with an artist until they have a record deal. Each manager is different.

For me? It depends. If I'm looking for someone and that person comes along, I'll get involved with them right at the beginning, before they step foot in a recording studio. It just depends at what point I am in my business.

If I'm looking to get involved in a new project and I'm kind of busy right now, then I'll be only interested in something that's established because I won't have the time right then and there to put into the development of a new act.

RANDY: How do you know if you've found a good manager or not?

JOHNNY: It comes down to whether or not you are successful.

RANDY: What do managers usually charge?

JOHNNY: There is no standard in the music business as to what a manager gets. It's whatever you and he negotiate and you feel is acceptable.

RANDY: What advice do you have for people starting out?

JOHNNY: To be as involved as you can in every aspect of your musical career. Be a writer, play an instrument. Be as in control of what it is you want to present to the public as possible. Be as self-contained in your own business as possible. People who want to get in the business and are willing to sign anything and be any kind of singer as they get on the stage will find out that their career will be short-lived. They will also find out with their first album that they're not happy with the artist that they've become.

If you are starting out and you know that your heart is in country and western music but you have an opportunity to join a boy band that does pop music and you are going to do that just to get into the music business, then that is the wrong reason to get into the music business. You have to be in the music business because you have a passion for the music that you want to do. Don't sell yourself out for opportunities. Twenty years from now, if you're still in the business, you'll respect yourself and you will love the artist you've become.

RANDY: You helped build some of the biggest acts of all time as a manager. Give me an example of how you helped one of them get where they are today.

JOHNNY: At one time I worked with Britney Spears. When I first started working with her, she had already gotten a record deal. Her attorney at the time was a friend of mine and he said he wanted her to perform live in front of an audience. He asked if I would put her in front of *NSYNC.

Anytime you put a female artist in front of an act that's made up of all males that generates primarily a female fan base that comes to the shows, that female opening act usually has a hard time.

The first time Britney opened for *NSYNC, as soon as she hit the stage, the girls started booing her. When she got through the 20-minute set, she got a lukewarm reaction. When she came backstage, I told her, "You have to make them feel like you are one of them and they are like you. When you go backstage, you're a threat to them because they think you're going to get together with one of the members of *NSYNC. "

So what I told her to say is, "I just came from backstage hanging out with my five big brothers and they're a little lonely back there. So I'm looking for five good girls who will be nice to my five big brothers. Is there anybody I can introduce to them?" Of course, the whole place went crazy, raising their hands wanting her to take them backstage.

She did that. After that, every girl wanted Britney to take them backstage to meet the guys. That took away the element of, "She's a threat to us." She became cool. And then they could focus in on the fact that, "Hey, she's a cool girl. She's a great singer. She's a great dancer and I really dig her songs."

From the time she started doing that, audiences started warming up to her.

RANDY: What are some other things you've done to make your artists so successful?

JOHNNY: You get together and basically consult and work hard and find opportunities and fight for your artist and sometimes even fight your artist to move in the right direction. People can get swayed and confused in this business. If you sit down and map out a game plan, and that's the game plan that you and your artist say that you want to take, sometimes you have to move your artist back onto that game plan because they can stray from it.

RANDY: What are common mistakes people make on the way up?

JOHNNY: One of the most common mistakes people make is to try to imitate somebody or something that is already successful in the music business, instead of trying to find originality in themselves and following that path. There are carbon copies of a lot of things out there, and once the original comes out, everything that comes out just like it is less successful. For me, I'm always looking to help manage artists who want to be original and want to move in a whole different direction than the flavor of the month.

Finding an agent

AGENTS ARE BASICALLY TALENT BOOKERS. THEY BOOK your shows and concerts nationally and locally. They keep you working. When your career starts to take off, an agency can help you get TV and commercial bookings and endorsements to help spread the word about you as an artist. They can do other things that can help you on your way.

Usually the agent is one of the last people you hire because you typically need one once you have it all together. You need an agent when you're trying to play serious shows and are about to go on tour and promote your album. But it depends. If you are a rock band that's just starting out and meet an agent who wants to book you locally, then you have an agent before you have a manager in this case. (But again, you need the lawyer to look over any contracts, Dawg.) There are no hard and fast rules, but usually anagent is hired later on.

To help you understand what an agent does, here's an interview with my friend Rob Light, a managing partner of Creative Artists Agency, one of the powerhouses in the business.

RANDY: So Rob, what does an agent do?

ROB: An agent is a member of an artist's overall team. If the manager is the quarterback of that team, or an essential part of that team, he then brings in specialists to help out in specific areas. He'll bring in a publicist to get the word out about this artist. He'll work with the record company to release and market the record. And he'll bring in an agent to help arrange bookings, live appearances, television appearances and concerts.

If you are a live performer and you intend to go on tour or do live gigs, whether locally to break in a band, regionally or nationally, your agent is who goes and gets you work. Your agent should have knowledge of the overall market and how best to present your genre of music. It's not just picking up the phone and calling someone and saying, "I have someone who wants to perform live in your club." The agent has to know the right rooms to play, when to play, what kind of deals to make, what ticket prices to charge. All of these factors lead to a perception of an artist or band, and those initial perceptions go on to form a foundation of a career.

The agent is responsible for all the live appearances that an artist does. Live appearances include everything from live television appearances to live concert appearances. We coordinate all of that, in conjunction with the label and publicist, to best use an artist's time and energy.

More than ever, touring is an integral part of breaking in an artist and developing an artist. Agents play a pivotal role in artist development.

RANDY: How should you go about finding an agent?

ROB: Your other representatives are starting to go out to agents and saying, "This is a rare, special talent and you need to be involved." If your career has enough energy going forward, then an agent wants to be involved.

It's not hard to find an agent if you're a great artist. It's hard when you're not talented. As we've seen on shows like *American Idol*, the difference between good and great can be as wide as the Grand Canyon. Being good isn't enough. Being great sometimes isn't enough. When you stand out and are special, it's not hard to find good people to work with. You can teach people to sing and dance, you can find great songs, you cannot teach charisma.

RANDY: What does an agent get paid?

ROB: Usually 10 percent of what the artist is being paid for his live personal appearances. In addition, we would usually be paid 10 percent of earnings in the area of sponsorship, film, soundtracks, television and books—all areas in which an agency works.

RANDY: What are some things to look out for when hiring an agent?

ROB: You want someone who understands your music and who is passionate about your music. You want someone who's got the time and the energy and the staff to work on your project. You want someone with vision, who sees more than just the next six months—who has the ability to lay out a plan and to use personal appearances and live shows to help you develop your craft and fulfill that vision.

RANDY: What advice do you have for people just starting out?

ROB: Someone just starting out needs to have a lot of patience and to be really honest with themselves about their talent, what they're good at and what they need to work on. I think the hardest thing is to be self-critical and invite the people you trust to give you honest criticism so you can grow. Having someone around who's saying, "You're great, you're great, you're great," does nothing. It's constructive criticism and honest evaluation that help you to grow.

RANDY: What are common pitfalls that up-and-comers often face?

ROB: Rushing into deals. Being seduced by the first thing that comes your way. Believing that it can happen overnight. The Cinderella story isn't reality. I'd say 99.9 percent of the people who have made it big have worked at it for a long time and have put a lot of sweat and tears and energy into becoming a success. This notion that you can go into the studio and cut a couple of demos and six months later you'll be on television playing Radio City Music Hall isn't reality. But I think that's the dream that fuels a lot of the people who get into this.

If you're getting into this because you want to be famous, you're getting into it for the wrong reason and chances are you'll never be successful. If you're getting into it because you love the art—you love to sing and perform and you love the craft and fame is not the central issue—you have a lot more going for you, and a lot more chance for success.

Business managers and accountants

WHEN YOU'RE GETTING STARTED AND DON'T HAVE TOO much cheddar in your bank account, you really don't need a business manager or accountant. You'll need one when you really start raking in the cha-ching and your financial affairs become more complicated.

Now you have a handle on what you should expect in this part of your career. As I said, you have to learn everything you can about the business side so that when people are talking to you, you understand them and you can make decisions from a position of strength and knowledge. This is why I encourage you to go to college.

But whether you go to college or not, you always need to do your own homework and research. It's your responsibility to always be prepared and find out everything you can about what you're involved in. Remember to always keep it real, baby.

Capturing the Holy Grail—
How to Score a
Record Deal

chapter seven

LET THE GAMES BEGIN. YOU'VE BEEN
HONING YOUR skills for a while and
have now reached the point where
you're trying to land the all-impor-
tant record deal so you can share
your talent with the entire known
world. You want your songs playing on the
radio from Santa Monica, California, to Portland,
Maine, and everywhere in between. You want to be on
MTV, VH1 and BET, the *Today* show, *Good Morning
America*, *The Early Show*, *Total Request Live*, *The Tonight
Show with Jay Leno* and the *Late Show with David
Letterman*, to start. You want the cover of *Rolling Stone*,
Vanity Fair, *Vibe* and *Source*. And of course, you want the
possibility of making mountains of cash. You wanna be
down.

Whoa. Not so fast. At this stage of the game, you want
to network like crazy with the industry's power players—or
with anyone who remotely knows them—to get them to lis-

ten to your demo and give you a shot. If you haven't done so already, you want to try to hire the best lawyer, producer and/or manager you can before you knock on the label's door. You need to understand just who does what inside a major label. You may also want to check out smaller labels or even go the independent route.

Make sure you are working with the A-Team

MAYBE YOU'VE HIRED A PRETTY GOOD LOCAL MANAGER and producer and you're working with a songwriter you really like. If your team hasn't already done so, you should have them reach out to contacts and major players in LA, New York, Nashville or even Atlanta, which is a growing music center.

At this point, you should know who the players are. If not, get to work. As I said in Chapter 5, you need to read magazines, newspapers and CD covers and surf the Internet to find out the names of the hottest producers, attorneys, managers, agents, songwriters and execs, as well as the up-and-comers. You should know who some of the biggest movers and shakers are in the industry: RCA Music Group Chairman Clive Davis, Def Jam President Kevin Liles, Island Def Jam Chairman Lyor Cohen, Interscope Geffen A&M Chairman Jimmy Iovine, Universal Music Group's Doug Morris and Aftermath's Dr. Dre, among many others. You should become so well-versed in these names that all of these names become second nature to you. Now you'll know who to contact to get where you want to go.

If you feel like your team is lining up good gigs and meetings with important people and is moving your career along, stick with them. But maybe the local team you've put together isn't getting anywhere. Your manager has mailed out your CDs to record companies and producers and gotten a bunch of form rejection letters, saying something like, "Sorry, this is not going to work for us at this time. Keep sending in your demos." Or maybe you spent months working on a demo, but the producer didn't quite achieve the sound you wanted.

There comes a point when you have to move on and find producers, songwriters and managers who have better connections and can really help you. You want to team up with the highest level of producers, songwriters and managers you can at this point. You know that you're probably not going to get red-hot producers like Jimmy Jam, Terry Lewis, Jermaine Dupri or Dr. Dre to help you with your demo. But since you've done your homework, you know who the A-, B- and C-level players are. You're going to aim for the B-level, if you can. If you can't get to B-level people, start with C-level people.

My guess is that you're probably working with D-level people in your hometown, which is the beginning level. The odds are that the songwriters, managers and producers in your hometown probably have never had any major success. If they haven't had any success, how are they going to help you? You want people on your team who are in-the-know. They need to be much smarter than you. If you're the smartest one in the room, get out of that room.

Pack your bags

IF YOU WANT TO MAKE BETTER CONTACTS, ONE option is to move to LA, New York or Nashville. Hey, if you're working at Krispy Kreme in Birmingham, Alabama, you can work at Krispy Kreme in LA while your career is getting started.

Sometimes taking the chance is worth it. Some people may disagree with this advice, but this is what worked for me. I did everything I could in my hometown of Baton Rouge, Louisiana, to pursue my dreams. But I knew I had to go elsewhere to further those dreams. I took everything in small steps, just like I'm telling you, dude. Most of the time, success is not going to come to you. You have to go to where the power centers are so the right people can see what you have to offer firsthand.

Network, network, network

I'M ASSUMING YOU KNOW NO ONE AT THIS point, or very few people in the business who can help you, so you have to work really hard at networking. Back in Chapter 5, I told you to start networking. Now's when you have to shift it into high gear. Whether you're working it in any of the big music centers or in your local area, hang out where people in the business hang out. Go to parties, clubs and every show in town to see if you can meet somebody who can help you connect with the people you need to know. Try to meet people backstage. Try to get to know the musicians connected with a well-known band you like. Talk to people who work at radio stations. Try to meet the staff of a well-known manager. A top producer's assistant. Roadies. A promoter.

But as I told you earlier, depending on where you're going, you may want to bring a buddy with you to watch your back. Be cautious. You don't want to get into situations that are over your head, Dawg.

You can also attend seminars and conventions across the country, such as the CMJ (*College Music Journal*) Music Marathon in New York City or the South by Southwest Music Conference in Austin, Texas. A&R people flood these conventions to hear up-and-coming acts play and to find new acts. New artists travel from all over the country to be discovered at conventions like these and others. You should check out one of these conventions to meet people who may be able to help you, to "sponge and learn" and see what kinds of music and acts record companies are excited about.

You should also find out who the key A&R people are on each label in your genre of music. This way, you'll be sending your demo to the right person. A&R people who sign hip-hop acts usually aren't looking at pop artists. Find out what kind of artists they've signed, what kind of music they like and which artists have been successful under their guidance.

Above all, you've got to learn how to be resourceful. Networking at this level is incredibly hard and often holds people back from not going further. Keep trying and keep it movin'.

Your own hit factory

EARLIER IN THE BOOK, I TALKED ABOUT HOW important a hit song is for landing a record deal, especially if you sing or play pop, R&B, country or a mix of these. If you don't have a hit song yet, this is your biggest hurdle right now. If the songwriter you're working with can't help you find a hit song, you've got to cut bait and move on. You've got to keep it moving until you find the people who can help you.

If I didn't mention it before, you should be living in the record store or surfing the Internet. (I love iTunes.) You can learn about new albums coming out, see what people are buying and do your own market research. If you are in a store or a chat room, you can ask people questions, like, "Why do you like this singer? Why don't you like that singer? Why are you buying that album? What do you think is hot right now?"

Knowing what is hot is one of the key questions for you now and for the rest of your career. You absolutely have to know what is going on in your genre. You need to ask yourself, "Am I competing with Justin Timberlake, Tool or Martina McBride? What are they doing? How can I do things differently? How should I package myself?"

Keep networking and meeting songwriters and the movers and shakers in the biz who can help you find that hit song. Don't stop until you find it.

You're a lot closer now

SO MAYBE YOU'VE MOVED TO A BIG CITY and gotten better contacts or found a new team. You hired a manager who knows more people. You're getting to know a more established group of songwriters. You're now working on your first, second or third demo. You have a following now when you play gigs. Keep booking those shows. This is a great way for record labels to hear about you.

Now you want to turn up the heat, dude. Give that demo to as many people as you can. Be tireless about it—but not a pain. You don't want to be so aggressive that you turn people off.

You have to repeat these steps many times, while continuing to rehearse and polish your craft. You've got to keep climbing up the ladder, networking and trying to reach your goal. You continue until a record company bites. And remember: hit song, hit song, hit song. Talent. Talent. Talent.

straight outta da Dawg's Mouth—*tip 16*

As I told you earlier, it's important to learn from the competition and pick up tips on what and what not to do from them. But you don't want to compare how you're doing with anyone else. This is about you and your journey. Comparing yourself to others can only deflate your psyche.

You might say, "One of my voice teacher's other students just got signed to a huge record deal. Why isn't this happening to me? I'm better than him."

Yo, somebody will always be better than you. And somebody's success will always happen quicker than yours. You can't be concerned with that. You can only be concerned with what you can do to succeed. While you're running this race, focus on your lane. Don't look to the side or in back of you. You have to take care of your own business, and that's how you'll be successful.

Getting to know the people at the labels

THE MAJOR RECORD COMPANIES INCLUDE:

- Warner Music Group, which includes Warner Bros. Records, The Atlantic Group, Elektra Entertainment Group and Sire Records Group

- Sony Music Entertainment, which includes Columbia Records Group and Epic Records Group

- Universal Music Group, which includes Def Jam, Island Def Jam, Universal Records, MCA and Geffen Records

- EMI Group, which includes Capitol, EMI and Virgin

- BMG Entertainment Labels, which includes Arista Records and RCA

At some point, A&R reps may want to meet you. They may talk to you backstage after one of your shows or they may call you into the office for a meeting.

You need to learn how to interview well. You need to be charming, interesting and on top of your game. You want them to like you. You want to connect with them. You want to make a good first impression. This lets them know how you will interview later with radio buyers and others.

You want to know what you are talking about. You should know everything about what you are doing musically. What your lyrics mean. The direction you're trying to go in as an artist. Who you think the hot producers are for your style of music.

A&R reps might ask you questions like: What would

you call the style of music you're performing? (Assuming that you are trying to do something unique and different . . .) What radio format do you think best fits your music? What producers and/or songwriters would you like to work with? Are you attached to your band and/or musicians?

If they ask you this, they're basically asking if you know what the weak links are in your band. Could you lose the so-so drummer or the writers you've been working with? How motivated are you to make changes to improve what you're doing if they have a better suggestion?

They may ask what your best song is. If they do, they're really asking whether you think you have a song that you think could be a hit. This tells them if you know what a hit is and where you are with finding one.

You are trying to figure out who you are and how you can sell your act in the marketplace. During an interview, the A&R rep is trying to figure out who they're working with and whether you can make it in the marketplace. Be blatantly honest with your answers. A&R reps know a lot more than you about what's going on and can see through any lies you tell them. Don't try to BS them.

You may want to prepare for any interviews that come your way. You don't want to sound dumb, which is not as cool as you might think. If you're a hip-hop kid, you may think that it's cool to sound elusive when someone asks a question by saying, "Yeah, you know what it's like." Or if you're with an alternative band, you might not talk much because you want to seem introspective.

These people are not your fans yet. You want to win them over. They want to see what kind of personality you have. They also want to know how well you know music.

When I was doing A&R, I could tell by asking a couple questions whether somebody knew what they were talking about and knew who they were. Once again, be prepared and sell yourself. You want that deal.

Courting the record company

MAYBE AN A&R REP FROM A MAJOR LABEL came to hear you at one of your many sold-out shows and called you in for a meeting. Or maybe your manager sent your demo to his old A&R buddy who just started working at a new label.

If you're courting a record company, your manager or attorney will help you deal with the execs there. Usually you'll be dealing with the A&R people first. If they have constructive comments, take them all in and think about how you can use them to improve.

Record execs may start coming to your shows and telling you, "We really like your band, but we don't like the songs." If they don't like the songs, then you have to go back to the drawing board and rework things.

As with anything, be careful about how you translate what they're telling you. If they keep saying, "I love you. I think you're great," and come to all your shows but never want to put any money down to sign you, either the person you're talking to doesn't have the power or is gassing you. Or there could be something that they're not telling you.

Read between the lines. There may be something they like about you or your act, which is why they keep coming back, but maybe something is off and that's what's holding them back.

Retrace your steps. Go over your performance again and again. Invite pros you trust to listen to you and tell you what they think could be wrong with your performance and then fix it. When you invite people to your shows, don't have them come just to hang out. Ask them to tell you what you need to change or what you could improve.

Capturing the Big Prize

LET'S SAY AN A&R REP GOT AHOLD OF your demo and is interested in you. You've been meeting with him or her and you find out the label wants to sign you. Cool, baby! All the practicing, networking and playing gigs while working a day job have paid off. Now is when that attorney becomes so valuable. He or she will now go over the fine print for you. Now your work is just beginning...

Reality check

DON'T START GETTING DELUSIONAL ON ME NOW. JUST because you've signed a deal doesn't mean you'll be a millionaire next week. So many people think, "Now that I've made a video, my record's going to soar! I'll be at the top of the charts. I wonder how I'll look on the cover of *Rolling Stone*. I'd better hire some bodyguards now because I'm definitely going to need them."

Scoring a deal, making an album or shooting a video does not always mean instant success. Even if you've made a video with Dave Meyers, one of the hottest video directors around, doesn't mean that BET and MTV will be knocking your door down.

Nothing is a guarantee. You may think, "My manager is best friends with the chairman of my label, so I'm all set. I don't have anything to worry about." Or "I've just hired Pink's accountant. Pink is rich, so I know I'll be rich." Chill, stay focused and get ready to work harder than you ever have.

Inside the record company

HERE IS A QUICK RUN-DOWN OF WHO does what at a label and what you need to know when you're first coming in the door.

After you meet with your A&R rep and the company is

ready to sign you, you may meet the president or chairman, who will sign off on the deal. The next possible people you'll meet may be in-house attorneys in the legal department, who will negotiate your deal with your lawyer and handle any other legal matters the company may face on your behalf.

After you get signed, you'll work with the A&R rep, who will help you make your album. At many companies, the A&R rep oversees the project. You and the A&R rep will discuss the direction of the record. The A&R rep will help put together the team of songwriters and producers who will work with you on your debut album and help you coordinate your recording budget. Along with the songwriters and the producers, the A&R rep will help you choose a recording studio, the musicians and backup singers you may need and your songs.

When all this is done, you will head into the studio with the producers. Recording costs for a band's first album can run from $250,000 to $500,000 or more. If you're a solo artist, recording costs can run from $350,000 to $1 million or more if you don't already have a band and they need to put one together for you.

After you make the album, all the other parts of the company take over. Your manager will usually accompany you to meetings and help you deal with each department as you work on releasing your record.

The marketing or product manager will figure out how to get your act into the marketplace. Marketing will put together a time line for the project: When will the first single be released? When will the video be released? When will the album come out?

Marketing will also work on putting together an advertising campaign for the album. They'll also figure out: Should we put this act on tour? Where? Who should this act tour with? Outkast or the Foo Fighters? Should they play Lollapalooza or do Ozzfest with Ozzy Osbourne? If you are going on tour, they may try to get sponsors and endorsements to offset promotional tour costs.

Working alongside marketing is the promotion department. Together with the chairman or the president of the label, the promotion department will help to choose the singles on your albums—the hits songs they plan to send to radio stations to get airplay for your music.

Every album ideally has two to three singles. The first single is the most important one and should be the best song on the record. You want to show the world how hot your album is with a blazing first single leading the way. A great single will make radio stations want to play the song and future fans want to buy it.

Since radio is one of the most important ways for people to hear your songs and learn about you, the promotion department also figures out which stations to send your songs to and which radio format is right for you—R&B, Top Forty, urban adult, alternative, rhythm crossover, etc.

But radio isn't the only game in town. Plenty of fans find out about new artists by reading about them in magazines, newspapers or on the Internet, or seeing and hearing them on TV. So early on, you may also begin working with the in-house publicist, who will line up interviews with local and national radio, TV, newspapers and magazines and on the Internet, to let the world know about you.

You'll also work with the art department, which will help you create your album cover and take photos, including those that will be used for publicity.

In some companies, the art department will help you to put your video together. Other companies have separate video departments. A video can cost anywhere from $100,000 to $1 million or more, depending on how hot you are or the kind of video you're going to make.

The sales and distribution departments work to get your record into stores like Tower Records and mass-market retailers like Wal-Mart and Target. They try to get big, splashy window displays and good positioning for your record inside the store. They want your record displayed prominently on racks when customers walk in, not buried in the back near the storage room. They want your song to be played in the store, which can also make people want to buy your album.

The business department and/or A&R administration will handle money—paying salaries, advances, etc.

The company may also hire independent promotion people, independent marketing people and independent publicists to help them get the word out about you.

When you start with these costs, and add in traveling for radio and TV shows and promotional events, clothes, stylists and your advance, the costs of making a first album can range anywhere from $1 million to $5 million or more. Now that's some cheddar, dude . . .

Timing is everything, especially in the music biz

WHEN YOU ARE GETTING READY TO RELEASE YOUR album, set-up time is extremely important. You start setting up an album for release three to six months beforehand to make the biggest impact you can with the public.

During the set-up time, the company tries to coordinate all newspaper, magazine, TV, Internet and radio interviews. The in-house publicist can start talking to journalists and others three months before an album is released. The publicist usually needs a three-month head start to arrange interviews, since many magazines have long lead times.

The promotion department starts arranging radio play months before the release of the album so your singles can get enough airplay. You want people to like your song so much that when the album drops, they can't wait to go out and buy it.

Labels usually release records from new artists in the first, second or third quarter—the first nine months of the year. Most established artists release records in the fourth quarter—just in time for the holiday season.

straight outta da $\mathcal{E}xpert's$ *Mouth*

So, yo. You wanna know where the record company is coming from? One of my big Dawgs, Kevin Liles, is president of Def Jam Records, a $400 million company, that houses the biggest stars in the hip-hop world, from Jay-Z and Ashanti to DMX and Ludacris.

RANDY: So Kevin, man, how hard is it to make it in the business today?

KEVIN: As hard as it is to get into the NBA or the NFL. If you're going to get into the game, you need a different mindset. Instead of going for a regular record deal, a lot of people today in the hip-hop world put up their own money and create their own record companies before coming to us.

But even though they do that, a lot of the times they just end up spending a lot of money and don't go anywhere else, because of a lack of experience. Everybody thinks it's all so easy. If you stop ten guys on the block, nine of them rap. A lot of them will go into a studio and rap, but if you count the ones who'll be on a label, be profitable and successful, there are only a handful of them.

RANDY: What's a company like Def Jam looking for these days?

KEVIN: At the end of the day, my mantra is to sign stars. Our job is to find those artists who will be significant to the hip-hop culture.

But I'm also looking for people who made things happen for themselves before they got to us. Starting in the early days with LL Cool J, Beastie Boys, Public Enemy to more recent signings of DMX, the Ruff Ryders' movement, Jay-Z, the Roc-a-fella movement, Ja Rule, Ludacris and the Def Jam South movement, all of these were spearheaded by entrepreneurs. These were guys who said, "I'm not just asking you to spend money on me. I want to spend my own money on me and try to become as successful as I can." I'm looking for stars with an entrepreneurial mindset.

I love the people who don't come to the record company to put out a record. They already put out their record. They're coming here to get more financing and to let the world know who they are.

That entrepreneurial spirit is why hip-hop has taken off today. Years ago, we would turn on the radio stations and they would play no rap. We would go buy clothes and they fit too tight. We wanted to listen to music that was different from our parents.' We saw that our community and our culture wasn't being serviced, so we took care of it ourselves. What happened a billion dollars later is that people realized how potent we are.

RANDY: So you're saying that people need to have themselves together when they approach your company.

KEVIN: If you want a used car you go to a used car lot. I'm not a used car lot. I'm the most potent brand in hip-hop. We're the Mercedes-Benz of the hip-hop world. We're not just going to accept any engine or any design. And we're going to have a lot of limited edition cars. Not everybody is going to be able to drive our cars.

RANDY: How hard is it to get a record deal today?

KEVIN: In the hip-hop world, it's easier to get a record deal if you put your own records out first and start a buzz, than it is to get a deal based on raw talent and nothing else. As I said, I'm interested in partners. I'm interested in entrepreneurs.

RANDY: What do the A&R people at Def Jam look for in up-and-comers?

KEVIN: We like to see that you already have a following in your area. We love to see a new artist already on the local radio station or have a CD that they're selling independently. We look for artists who, when you go to their hometown and they perform, the whole crowd goes crazy. If you're not hot where you're from, how do you think I'm going to promote you around the country?

If you're just getting started, my advice is to look, listen and learn. Another thing is that today's market is so competitive and so abundant—there are so many rappers, singers, producers, that you have to differentiate or die.

RANDY: What do all of the stars at your company have in common?

KEVIN: All of them are able to adapt to change. They all transcend the music. People want to be like them, want to act like them and wear what they got on. When they walk into a room, everybody stops.

RANDY: What do you do as president of Def Jam?

KEVIN: I broker deals, go to finance meetings, go to the studio, work on financial reports, get into new businesses, get rid of old businesses and protect the brand.

I also do whatever is necessary. If I see a piece of garbage on the floor when I'm walking, I pick it up, so in that sense, I'm the janitor. If I have to go in the studio because I have an idea for an artist, then I'm an A&R person. If I call the radio station, I'm a promotions person. I do whatever is necessary to get the job done.

What I do goes beyond the business end. I am employed by a company. But I feel like I represent a culture. I don't even look at our company as a record company. We change lives.

RANDY: What are some of the biggest pitfalls you see in people coming up?

KEVIN: Lack of desire, high expectations and low work ethic. It all boils down to this: How much do you want it and what are you willing to sacrifice to get it? If I'm going to roll out a single that costs me $1.5 to $2 million, then what are you going to do to help it along? Any true superstar who is going to put forth that entrepreneurial spirit will have great success in the hip-hop world, at least.

But if you're willing to work hard and you have the talent, you could go all the way.

I would say that the great thing about our business and America is you can have nothing today and be something tomorrow. Everyone is not an American Idol, but everyone has that American opportunity.

My boy, Jeff Fenster, is senior VP of A&R at Island Def Jam Music Group. He can fill you in on what A&R reps look for. He is a 23-year veteran of the business who was a music attorney for eight years and has been in A&R for 15 years. He was the head of A&R at Jive Records for seven years and has been at Island Def Jam for the past four years. He has signed or A&R'd artists including Britney Spears, the Backstreet Boys, R. Kelly, A Tribe Called Quest and Sum 41.

RANDY: So Jeff, what does an A&R person do?

JEFF: An A&R person finds great talent. He or she convinces that artist to sign with their company as opposed to some other company and then sometimes gets involved in the parameters of the deal itself.

Then the A&R person adds whatever the artist needs to make a great record. Often that means finding a producer, engineer, mixer, sometimes musicians or bands, as well. And then it often involves finding either songwriting collaborators for the artist or the songs themselves, if the artist doesn't primarily write his or her own songs.

Finding songs for an artist is one of the classic roles of an A&R person. A&R stands for Artists and Repertoire, because traditionally in the business, artists didn't write their own songs. Now artists often write their own material. But still, in many cases, A&R people help artists find the great songs they need. Even if the artist writes his or her own songs, the A&R person may make suggestions on how to improve the songs and help choose which songs will be put on the album and which ones will be singles.

Those are the basics. Any great A&R person stays involved in all aspects of realizing the artist's vision even after the record is made. That means staying involved in the artist's development, such as getting the artist ready to do a great live show or to deal with the media, or working with management or the agent to help find touring opportunities. An A&R person will be involved in the videos and all aspects of the marketing plan to make sure the artistic vision is realized every step along the way. An A&R person will most importantly be the person who communicates that vision to all aspects of the company and acts as both a cheerleader and a communicator of the artistic vision on behalf of the artist and management to the entire record company.

RANDY: What do you look for as an A&R exec?

JEFF: As an A&R person, I've never concentrated on what's hot at any given moment. By the time you sign an artist and make an album, which is a process that often takes a year or more, whatever was hot at that moment that you signed the artist may not be hot when the record comes out.

In addition, whatever is hot may mean that it's a crowded lane—that there are already artists who are doing that kind of music. I always try to look for the less traveled lanes.

There are a number of things I look for as an A&R person. The criterion I look for are great songs. Songs are the key to our business. Sometimes you find an artist you think is great and can be successful who doesn't bring in the songs themselves initially, but that is a key factor. I look for musical talent and ability, whether it's singing or musicianship or even dancing, in some cases. I also see if the artist has a perspective—some kind of unique point of view that sets them apart from other artists and the ability to touch and move people emotionally.

I also look for desire, commitment and focus, which are very important. I think every successful artist I've worked with has been extremely driven and wanted to succeed. I look for a good team—a good manager, agent and lawyer. I also look for marketability—that you can see a way that this artist will reach people and sell records, because when you are working for a major record company, you do have to sell records along the way.

RANDY: How do you get A&R people to notice you?

JEFF: Exposure is the key. It's easier than ever to make a home-created CD or to get a CD made in an inexpensive recording studio, whether you sing or play hip-hop, alternative music, rock or even pop. You sell that CD locally or try to get it on the radio locally. You can gain exposure through live performing, whether you're in a band that's getting a good draw locally or regionally or whether you're a pop artist or an urban artist who manages to open up for an established artist or perform at a noteworthy charity event or singing the national anthem for sporting teams. Any kind of exposure is a potential avenue to somebody noticing you. Not everybody can win *American Idol*, but there are a lot of ways to get exposure short of 30 million people at a time watching you.

Even though it's easier for people to make their own CDs, you can still go the traditional route and make a demo. You can still make a basic, good-quality demo and get it to people in the industry, especially if it's pitched by a reputable manager, lawyer, producer, booking agent, or even a journalist.

The key is to get some kind of experience and try to get to anybody who is a credible person in the business, even if it's not specifically an A&R person, because we are always looking for new material from our contacts.

Sending something cold to record companies doesn't get you anywhere. A lot of record companies still don't take unsolicited demos. You have to get somebody's attention.

I don't think you have to be in New York or LA to make things happen. But you do have to get somebody in LA or New York to notice you, even if it's through somebody who's in the business wherever you are.

RANDY: You have worked with some of the biggest artists of all time, from R. Kelly to Britney Spears. Talk about what you saw in, say, Britney Spears when you first learned about her.

JEFF: With Britney, I got a one-song demo and some pictures and then I brought her in for a meeting at my office. It was the meeting that clinched it for me. I saw that she had the most intense focus and desire that came from her, not from her parents or anyone else. She'd had it since she was a little girl. I was impressed with her drive and commitment, coupled with musical talent and an extremely appealing personality. She was only 15 at the time. She was good looking, but there was something more about her. She had warmth. She was the kind of person you root for.

RANDY: What other advice do you have for up-and-comers?

JEFF: Besides what I said earlier, have a communicable vision for what you want to say and also an idea of who your audience is. People in my position appreciate artists who have a sense of themselves both in terms of their music and in terms of who their intended audience is. Know what you want to say and who you want to speak to.

Music lawyers can be helpful because they can shop something for you. They are a source of a lot of our demos. Britney Spears, the biggest artist I ever signed, came from a lawyer. But even when you start to get interest from companies, it's important to have a good lawyer to protect you and make sure you don't get taken advantage of.

RANDY: What pitfalls do people starting out often face?

JEFF: A mistake people often make is thinking that they can shortcut any of these things I've been talking about. This journey is a process that takes a long time. Shortcuts usually don't exist.

Be careful of production deals. They are good if they're with the right party, someone who's reputable. They're often 1,000 times worse than a major record company deal is, in my opinion.

RANDY: Any other words of wisdom?

JEFF: Remember that as daunting as it sounds, the deal is just the beginning. I would say that more than 90 percent of the artists who get signed to major record companies still are not successful.

And don't forget great songs. It's all about songs.

When it comes to doing publicity for superstars in the music industry, Liz Rosenberg is the platinum standard. Liz has been doing publicity for Warner Bros. Records for 32 years and reps superstars like Madonna, Cher, Fleetwood Mac, Josh Groban, k.d. lang, Chris Isaak and Eric Benét among others. She has also repped Prince, Bette Midler, Rod Stewart, Bonnie Raitt, George Harrison, the Pretenders, Chaka Khan, Faith Hill and Jimmy Cliff.

RANDY: When you've just signed a deal, what will an in-house publicist do for you?

LIZ: An in-house publicist or press agent (as I like to describe it) does publicity exclusively for artists who record for the label. Their job is to get the word out about an artist and their music through newspaper, magazine, TV, radio and Internet interviews and record reviews. As a press agent, your job is to find outlets that work for the kind of music the artist creates.

You start by trying to get a buzz going within the industry and the media about the artist and the music so people start anticipating the eventual release of the product. You introduce the artist and their music to the media. You help them formulate the messages they want to convey to the public about their music. You work with them on how they are going to describe their music, anything else they want to talk about, how to be engaging and how to tell their story. You help them express themselves in an eloquent way. Some people have a lot of trouble describing their music.

They can make the music, but they have a hard time putting it into words.

Sometimes publicists will hire media coaches to work with artists. I usually spend time talking to the artist, sitting in on interviews and helping them as they go along.

An in-house press agent usually meets an artist or a group and their manager right before they're signed or shortly thereafter. The in-house publicist explains how the company works and how they're going to work with the artist.

Most of the publicity would obviously be based around the release of the artist's first album. A press agent will start working on a bio, which would essentially tell the artist's background story. The press agent would also start working on arranging photo shoots for publicity purposes.

Photos are important. When I am going to be introducing a new artist to magazines or journalists or photo editors or anyone who could be helpful in getting the word out about that artist, I need to have some artwork to show them.

Visuals are important for an artist. Ideally you would like it to only be about the music, but it isn't. The artist is going to have to do magazine and newspaper interviews, which may run pictures, as well as TV appearances, so you have to start by at least being able to show what an artist or a group looks like.

There's a lot of educating that a press agent has to do with a new artist at the beginning. I try to explain some of the realities about the media and what they might expect and what is realistic for them to expect as new artists. There are new artists who were signed who say, "I want to be on the cover of *Time* magazine. Why aren't I?" or "I want a good review in this magazine," or, "I hate this newspaper." If an artist says, "I don't want to do this magazine because it's not cool," if I think differently, I have to convince them why they should do it.

RANDY: If you just got signed, what tips do you have for making the artist/publicist relationship work well?

LIZ: Ask questions. Be respectful. Develop a friendship if possible. The relationship between an artist and press agent is very intimate. They tell you their troubles. You get them to a throat doctor. You find them the socks they need for a TV show. You get involved with their families. It isn't always that way but seems to be that way for me, more often than not. It's quite a close relationship and it goes on for a very long time, so it's important to establish a healthy relationship at the beginning.

The press agent also acts a little bit as your representative within the company, which is an advantage to having an in-house press agent. An in-house publicist can help spread the artist's message internally. They can rev up the company about you. If they hear a song of yours that is really great, they can give feedback to the rest of the company about the kind of response you are getting out in the world.

If I go to *Rolling Stone*, for example, and play Josh Groban's new record and the editor goes crazy and loves it, this is information I can bring back to the company that will hopefully inspire them to make a further commitment to the artist as far as marketing or promoting their music.

RANDY: What do you do as a publicist before a new artist's first album is released?

LIZ: For a new artist especially, the set-up of an album is such an important component. I can't just send a CD to newspapers and magazines and TV shows the day it's coming out and expect there to be any momentum, even if it's a great record. I'll start talking to journalists about a new album sometimes three months before it comes out.

Before doing so, I try to find out as much as I can about the album and the artist. I may go into the studio to hear the artist recording. Sometimes I'll meet with an artist and he'll tell me what he's doing or he'll show me lyrics he really likes.

If an artist comes to me at 10 o'clock in the morning and says, "Let me play you a song I wrote last night," and I am completely knocked out about how great it is, in the course of many conversations in my day, I will pass that information onto the journalists and TV bookers I talk to all day long. I might say, "I just heard this new artist the company signed. He is incredible. I never heard lyrics like this before." It just plants the seed. So a week later when I say, "Remember that single I was talking about? I've got to send you a copy."

Or I may see the results of a publicity photo shoot and think this artist would be perfect for a magazine like *GQ* or *Blender* or *Vibe*. I might talk to a music editor and say, "I have some great pictures of this new artist. I'll send over the pictures. He's cute and he's making a really great record."

RANDY: I'm sure you've faced many challenges when doing publicity for the stars you rep. Talk about one of the challenges you've faced in your career and how you overcame it.

LIZ: When I started working with Madonna in 1982, she made dance music—disco, which was not very popular with the press at the time. She was blonde. They thought she was stupid. There was little interest in this new artist no one had ever heard of. Nobody cared about her. I couldn't turn anyone on to her music. She had a singles deal at the time with Warner Bros. Records. The company was going to release two of her singles, and if they were successful, they were going to put out an album.

I believed in her from the moment I met her. This is an artist who came to my office in 1982 and lit up the room like a Christmas tree. She was so broke we would have to give her money to take the subway. But I just found her unbelievably enchanting. I loved her drive and her spirit and mostly thought the music was amazing. I just said, "I'm going for this." And the rest, of course, is musical legend.

You have that feeling when someone comes into your office for the first time. I'm not always right, but if an artist can inspire a press agent on any level, it helps so much. You don't have to be a Christmas tree. You could just make incredible music. If you help the press agent become a believer and a fighter for you, then you have made the best first step possible in your career as an artist with the media.

Even though I loved Madonna and felt she was a star, I still had tremendous difficulty getting people to pay attention to her. She started having some success on the radio, which helped me get my foot in the door publicity-wise. I was pitching tons of journalists and finally found a music writer with a dance background who was interested in writing about her for *Newsday*. It was a big article on Madonna, so I tried to use that story to try to get more press for her. I called the producers of TV shows and no one wanted to book her. I would beg them. But no one wanted to take a chance.

The only answer is to persevere and hope that one person gets what you're saying and will take a chance and go with someone who is not a big star. Slowly but surely it started to build up.

Her success on the radio kept getting bigger and bigger. I convinced *Harper's Bazaar* to do a fashion story on her. Then *Rolling Stone* agreed to put her on the cover. I said, "OK. We've got it made. We're there." I thought we had reached the moment we had been waiting for.

Then the story came out. It was essentially a story about how Madonna had "allegedly" slept her way to the top. I was devastated. I thought it was going to end her career before it even got started—and thought that many times at the beginning of her career. It wasn't that I didn't believe in her. I just felt protective and wanted everything to go just right. I thought it was all going to go downhill from there because of this story.

But the story had the opposite effect. It polarized people. Controversy around Madonna started to grow. People couldn't stop talking about her. "Is she for real? Isn't she for real? Is she fabulous? Is she full of s——? Is she making a strong point about women being allowed to be sexual and be proud of it and have brains or is it the media whipping it up into a frenzy?"

The debate about Madonna became enormous in the media. It all went back to that article and whether they were taking the writer's side or Madonna's side. His implication was that she had minimal talent and slept her way to the top. Obviously, most people believed in Madonna.

This was a great lesson for me as a press agent. I learned to just keep going. I believed in Madonna when nobody did and when no one wanted to write about her. I just knew in my heart and soul that she would reach a level that very few artists would ever reach. The Madonna success story developed a life of its own.

RANDY: What advice do you have for new artists who are dealing with publicists for the first time?

LIZ: I often tell them to read a lot of magazine and newspaper articles about artists because it can help them see what works and what doesn't. They also need to accept that no press agent can control what the media does. But we certainly try our best.

My advice is to show a press agent that you're willing to listen and that you're willing to work hard. The artist with the best work ethic is the one who has the best chance of succeeding. It is not just going to come to you. Making the music is half the battle, I think. Putting the work in, whether it's traveling all over the world going to as many countries as you can to have your music heard or whatever else needs to be done, that's what I call a dream artist.

Radio guru John Ivey can tell you all about how important radio is for anyone trying to make it in the music business. John is VP of programming for Clear Channel Radio in Los Angeles and Riverside, California. As part of his duties, he is the program director at KIIS-FM, the highest-billing Top Forty radio station in the country and at KYSR (Star 98.7), where *Idol*'s Ryan Seacrest is afternoon drive host.

RANDY: How hard is it to get radio airplay?

JOHN: It's very hard to get radio airplay. At each station, the program director and music director must be convinced that the song is something their target listeners will like. Picking the right music for their stations is one of the things the PD's and MD's need to do to increase the ratings on their stations. With tons of new music to choose from each week, it becomes very competitive when we decide what new music to add on to each station.

RANDY: What does it take for a song to become a hit?

JOHN: A great hook is key for a hit song. A part of the song that people can remember easily and end up hearing over and over in their heads. When somebody comes up to you and says, "I can't get this song out of my head" . . . that's a good thing!!!

RANDY: How do you decide what goes on the air?

JOHN: Each week I sit down with my music director at each station and listen to the new music that we feel is in contention for the week.

This music is pared down from all the new music we get in during the week, plus the music that has come in during the past few weeks that we have not yet decided to play. Only a very small portion of all the new songs that come into the station ever get airplay.

On the average, stations only play two or three new songs each week. That leaves tons of music each week that came in . . . but didn't make it. You determine how much new music you have the space for that week and then find the songs you feel your listeners will like best, taking into consideration tempo and texture of the song and genre (rock, pop, dance, ballad, alternative) if you are a Top Forty station.

RANDY: Where do you get your songs from? Major labels only?

JOHN: We get new music each week from everyone from the major record companies and local and independent record companies to individuals.

RANDY: How often do you play songs from independent producers?

JOHN: This depends on the song. Most songs that are really good get picked up quickly by major record companies.

RANDY: What advice do you have for people just starting out who are making demos or trying to get a record deal?

JOHN: Keep plugging away. Write a lot and play your music for people other than your family and friends. Take criticism. Play in public as much as possible to become a performer, not just a singer. Stay grounded. No "star" trips. Some of the biggest names in the industry are great people who love the business and work hard even after years of success. I have had easier dealings with people like Elton John, Michael Jackson, Celine Dion and Madonna than I have had with some artists who have had half a hit who think they are "the new thing" or "a STAR." When you finally get a record deal . . . that's when the work BEGINS!

Be prepared to work hard. Don't lose touch with reality. Don't surround yourself with "YES" people. Don't believe your own bulls——. Be thankful you have talent. One hit single or CD does not make a career. Ever heard of "one-hit wonders"? It's a roller coaster ride, but with patience and talent . . . it's a lot of fun. Remember, you're doing this for the music FIRST.

Here are a few other things to remember once you've signed a record deal.

You're not done networking

SO NOW YOU HAVE A DEAL. WELL, I'M sorry to tell you, but it's still not time for chillin'. All the networking you've been doing has to continue. You want to get to know as many people inside the label as possible because you need to have allies within the company.

Your main ally is an A&R person who really believes in you and is genuinely honest with you. And you still want to find other pros who are going to keep it real with you and tell you the truth. You want to put out the highest-quality album you can. This album can make or break your career. You don't want to have to stop just after you started.

So keep getting to know people. Find people in the company or in the industry you can trust.

Keep improving

AS YOU PREPARE TO MAKE YOUR FIRST ALBUM, try to have open, honest discussions with your A&R people and others at the label. If they think you still need voice lessons, keep taking them. If they think you need dance lessons, get moving.

Remember that you can always improve. I don't care what age you are or how big a star you are. I don't care if you've sold 18 bazillion records. Never think that you've arrived. When you do that, you usually stop trying.

Small labels

YOU DON'T HAVE TO START WITH THE BIGGEST labels on the planet. You may choose to go with a smaller independent label. There are hundreds of them out there. A smaller label may give you more attention than you would receive at a much bigger company. You may also get a deal faster at a small independent label.

But it may be harder to reach the masses with your music when you're working with a smaller company that doesn't have all the resources a larger company may have. You may make slower progress than you would at a major label. These are the things only you can weigh. You have to decide for yourself which is better for you.

As I've told you throughout this book, do your research. Find out about bands that have become successful by signing with smaller labels. Check out the labels you're interested in to see who they've worked with. Meet people who have gone with a smaller label and ask them about the pros and cons. It's an option worth exploring.

The independent route

YOU CAN ALSO TRY TO GO IT ALONE. There are legendary stories about bands that made things happen on their own. Blink 182, the Dave Matthews Band, Hootie and the Blowfish, Master P and the Ying Yang Twins all started their own parties.

When major labels came knocking, these acts had much more leverage than when they were unknowns, and they ended up with far better deals than they would have gotten otherwise.

If you want to go the independent route, you can produce your own CD. You can hitch a U-Haul trailer to your pickup or SUV and travel from city to city, trying to get your record played on local stations. You can set up shows everywhere, sell your CD there and on the Internet.

This is a hard route to travel but, as you've seen, it can be done. If you're good enough, people will pay attention. Still, it's not going to work for everyone.

straight outta da *Expert's Mouth*

My man Bruce Flohr can tell you all about the independent route. Bruce is a 15-year A&R veteran of RCA Records. While working there, he was responsible for many acts, including the Dave Matthews Band and Foo Fighters. He now works for ATO records and Red Light Management, which are both affiliated with the Dave Matthews Band.

Bruce also put in a good word for me when they were looking for *Idol* judges. Thanks, dude.

RANDY: So Bruce, how exactly did the Dave Matthews Band use the independent route to go from playing gigs in their hometown to headlining a concert in Central Park in New York City last summer for 100,000?

BRUCE: When the band first started out, they toured in unconventional places to build their fan base. They sometimes played several gigs a day—anything from a regular gig to a frat party to an after-prom party.

They weren't heavily pursuing any deals. They definitely had a demo floating around, but they weren't banging on people's doors to the point where they got frustrated. Some labels had heard it and passed, but no one really had ever stepped out of New York or LA to see these guys play until the spring of 1992.

At the time, I was working at RCA in Los Angeles doing A&R. An intern of mine from Colgate University came into my office and played me a tape of Dave playing acoustic in a coffee shop. It is because of that intern that I listen to every CD, whether it's from my next-door neighbor's best friend's uncle or from the most high-powered attorney in the music business, because you never know.

By the time Peter Robinson, a colleague of mine, and I went down to see the band, they had a huge following. They were playing to 500 kids in a club in New York and could consistently sell out small clubs up and down the East Coast.

We talked to them about signing with RCA. But the band's vision was, "We want to put out an independent record before we sign with a major label." We at RCA agreed with that vision and decided to help them market that record.

The deal with RCA almost didn't happen. As we courted them for a period of seven months, they got bigger and bigger and started to think maybe they didn't need us at all. What finally convinced them to do the deal was that we were very supportive of the independent record and we didn't discourage them from doing it.

They made the record and distributed it. We just guided them on where to put ads and where to take it to radio. We worked very much behind the scenes. The label thought it was a good idea because we needed to learn about their fan base. This independent record gave us that opportunity.

They sold 70,000 copies of their independent album, *Remember Two Things*, which was a live recording of them playing on stage.

Then they put out an album with RCA called *Under the Table and Dreaming*.

RANDY: How much has the industry changed because of artists who have gone independent?

BRUCE: The business is shifting. Major labels are going through a redefining of who and what they are. Artists, managers and even labels are getting frustrated because major companies are so big that they can't move quickly enough. When you are an independent, working by yourself, you can go play a show and if that doesn't work, you don't go back again. You know it immediately.

With a major label, sometimes it takes you four weeks to realize it didn't work because of the amount of information coming in. There are exceptions to the rule. But the majority of them are realizing they are too big to react as quickly as they need to.

As an artist on the independent level, you need to know what it's like to get your song on the radio, to get your CD in the record store or to get booked in a club. So when you give up those powers to other people, you know how difficult their job is and you know when they're doing it right or when they're doing it wrong.

RANDY: What advice do you have for people who want to go the independent route

BRUCE: Going independent is unfortunately becoming one of the only avenues left at this point, prior to signing to a major label. If you are strictly a pop band and it's all about radio, then sing your butt off and make the best song you can on your demo. If you are a performer, if you live and breathe it and love it so much that you don't care about making money, go the independent route for as long as you can.

This means starting at the grass-roots level. Growing it locally. Keeping the amount of people involved in your music small. Handpicking every person including your band members. It means that everybody has to have the same vision as you.

To Idol or Not to Idol . . .

THUS SPEAKETH THE DAWG. SO HERE YOU ARE. You've come this far. Now you're trying to decide, should I audition for a reality TV show like *American Idol* or *Star Search* or just go for a record deal? What are the pros and cons?

You and your team may feel that you have what it takes to make it right here and now. You may be working with A- or B-list producers, managers, attorneys and songwriters. You may have made your ninth demo and feel like the tenth will be the one that hits. There may be a lot of heat on you right now. Labels may be coming to your shows. Producers and songwriters may be hounding you. You might be right around the corner from a record deal. If this is the case, then you may not need to go the reality TV show route to clinch a deal.

But maybe the opposite is happening. Maybe you're having trouble getting your career off the ground. You can't find a good manager. No hot producers will take your calls.

The label is sending you rejection letters because they didn't like your demo—again. If you need extra help or if you are trying to figure out a different way to make it, one of the great new avenues is the reality TV show route.

Unlike trying to get a deal with a major label, you don't need to show up with a hit song when you *Idol* or do other reality TV. You come to the audition with that unbelievable talent you've been grooming, your uniqueness and your "itness" blazing.

The catch? You have to be able to do this on national TV in front of millions, for months, getting your groove on every time. If you can take the heaps of ridicule and the abuse that may come your way on the show from the judges, then go for it. If you're secure enough in yourself and in your talent, like others you've seen win, à la Kelly and Ruben, who won in the first two seasons, then you may want to get in line the next time *Idol* holds auditions.

Striking reality TV gold

WHEN *IDOL* OR ANOTHER MUSICAL TALENT SEARCH SHOW works its magic, contracts get signed. Records are made. Onetime wannabes become stars. Kelly and Ruben, Clay and Justin, Tamyra and Kimberly Locke are among the contestants who snagged major record deals after appearing on the show.

These kids are rockin'. Kelly's single, "A Moment Like This," debuted at number one. Her album, *Thankful*, went platinum. She was nominated for three MTV Video Music Awards, including best new artist, best pop video and viewers' choice.

Clay's single, "This Is the Night," debuted at number one. The last single that sold this many copies was Elton John's "Candle in the Wind." His debut album went double-platinum in the first week.

For these people, their choice to *Idol* was a good one. I think it would have been hard for them to get a record deal otherwise. Why? The powers-that-be in the music business—especially at labels—usually want everything brought to them. Record honchos weren't going to be in Alabama looking for Ruben or in a little town in Texas trying to discover Kelly. For any of the *Idol*ers to have landed deals, they would have had to make contact with the powers-that-be at the labels and in the business.

Let's put it this way. None of these six were penciling in meetings with Clive Davis or Johnny Wright before they got to *Idol*. None of the winners came to the audition with that ever-elusive hit song. None of them had the true record label look that companies tend to like, except for maybe Justin and Tamyra. Looks aside, record companies still wouldn't have signed any of them.

I'll bet that some companies don't like the fact that a show like *Idol* has become a monster success. We're traipsing on territory they think they own. Shows like *Idol* have proven record companies wrong by not going to them first, but taking the music straight to the people. You, the public, have chosen the winner each year. And you, the public, chose talent over everything else. For that, I stand and applaud you and kiss the ground. Thank God the public gets it because music is really for the people and not for the industry.

Put that thick skin to use

WHEN YOU HOOK UP WITH A LABEL, THE world may not see you for a year or two while you're busy making your album. Once you put your record out, the label will slowly introduce you to the world. You'll have time to grow.

It's the complete opposite on a reality TV show. From day one, all your strengths and weaknesses are broadcast in neon lights to the world, before you've even won the chance to make a record. You may think it's cool to be on TV, but once you step before those cameras, you won't be able to hide a thing. If you win the prize, your life will become a whirlwind of interviews, recording sessions and high-profile gigs. Nonstop. You'll suddenly have fans—everywhere you look. Instant fame can be tough for a newbie to handle at first.

You also need nerves and persistence of steel to audition for a show like *Idol*. Paula, Simon and I always say on the show that we're going to try to keep it real with you. So if you're going to stand before us, make sure that you're aware of every flaw and every strength in your character, performance and vocal abilities. Trust me. Each of us comes to the table with more than 25 years of experience in the music business. Simon has been a longtime record exec with BMG Records in England. He co-created the *American Idol* franchise. Paula was an artist with Virgin Records. I am a songwriter, musician, producer, manager and was a record executive for 13 years. We see *everything* and, as you know, won't hesitate to tell you all about it.

So Dawg, if you don't want everyone from your friends and family to the guy at the corner deli where you get your coffee every morning to hear what we honestly think of you on national TV, then going the reality TV show route is not for you. Everyone in the world knows that Simon didn't like Jim Verraros' singing on the first season of *Idol* when he told him, "I think if you win this competition, we will have failed." And you know what happened to Keith from Atlanta and countless others.

And if you're going to lash out and call us stupid names, then all I have to say to you is, "If you're gonna dish it, you gotta be able to take it."

A question I get asked all the time

YOU MAY REMEMBER THE MOMENT IN THE FIRST season when Simon and I almost came to blows over R.J. Helton, who was in the Top Ten on Idol's first season. R.J. had just finished singing "I'll Be There." I told R.J. I loved the sound of his voice. Paula told him his performance was solid.

Simon disagreed. He said he thought the performance was average. Then he got personal. "In the last two episodes . . . two losers have been voted through for one reason and one reason only," he said. "It is the sympathy vote and has nothing to do with talent."

I thought Simon went too far. I told him, "I've been sitting here week after week, and you keep insulting these people. You can't call people losers."

He shot back, saying, "I can call them whatever I like."

"No, you can't," I said. "This is America. We don't do this to people. We don't insult people like this."

We kept going round and round until finally I stood up

and said, "Hey, come on. You want to do something about it?" I didn't like him being that harsh with some of the kids. You can insult someone's singing, but that's where you have to draw the line. You can say, "Your singing sucked," but I *don't* want to hear someone call a contestant we don't really know a loser. I want to keep it specific to the talent. Otherwise, it's not fair.

We had words about it after the show. It took us a while, but we finally worked it out. Later on, I laughed when I heard that Simon said he didn't want any trouble with me. I don't blame him. That would be like Tom Green fighting The Rock, you know, man?

Now people think we're not friends. The reality? Simon, Paula, *Idol* host Ryan Seacrest and I are all really close. Simon and I got beyond our differences and are really good friends. Sometimes in life you need a little shakeup to learn to respect each other and learn how to really vibe.

Simon, Ryan and I hang out all the time. When we're doing the show, we have a Thursday night boys' club where we meet each week at different restaurants in town and chill. Paula and I have been friends for 15 years. We're working on some interesting projects together.

But yes, there have been other tense moments. The show is very emotional. We all have strong opinions about contestants. Nigel Lythgoe and Ken Warrick, the show's producers, told me early on, "As the show approaches the end of the season, you'll become attached to a lot of these kids. You're pulling for them because you believe in them and you want them to really win."

Man, they weren't lying. When Kelly, Ruben and Clay stood on stage at the end, I felt like a proud parent. In a cheesy, sentimental, corny way, I felt that I had done something good in the world: I helped somebody with amazing talent get their shot at the Big Time because they deserved it. Yo, now that's the way you get down.

Different strokes

THE THREE OF US COME AT JUDGING FROM three different places, which makes the show a lot of fun. Simon has more of a bludgeon-them-over-the-head style of commentary. He blasts people with his bruising honesty. Most of the time, his comments are truthful, but as we all know, they can be somewhat embarrassing and harsh at the same time. I know the truth hurts sometimes, but does it have to hurt that bad? He fires barbs like a harsh drill sergeant. Most people who encounter him figure, "I'm going to quit now."

Paula has the softest side of all of us. She's very sympathetic and really cares about the well-being of the people who come to see us. A lot of times she'll offer words of encouragement. Paula is always real warm to the kids.

So I guess that puts me in the middle. Like Simon and Paula, I definitely keep it real with the contestants. I try to give my honest opinion and share whatever wisdom I've gotten in 25 years. Sometimes I can be a little stinging with my commentary. Please understand, I'm not trying to kill or discourage any dreams. I just want to be honest when judging what's going on. If I think words of encouragement will help them, I'll offer them. If they suck, then I'll tell them. I don't want to give anybody any false hopes.

But I want to be on the side of the talent, cheering it

along. When I see contestants, I always feel that I'm looking at myself, because I was where you are at one point in my life. I have auditioned for tons of things. Some I won. Some I didn't get. Everything I'm telling you to do in this book is what I've experienced myself. Trying to become an artist. Trying to be a performer. I understand where you are coming from.

One more thing: Sometimes on the panel you may hear somebody, like Simon or Ryan, say, "We don't understand a word Randy's saying." If you watch BET, MTV and VH1, you'll hear people talking just like me. If you're in-the-know, cool and hip, you'll know what I'm talking about. I can't help it if I'm large, dope and in charge. I'm speaking the people's language, baby!

A hard's day's Idoling

WHEN WE'RE AUDITIONING PEOPLE, IT'S ALWAYS HARD WORK, fun and a bit surreal all at the same time. During the auditions, Paula, Simon and I spend a couple days in each city, seeing about 75 to 85 or more kids a day.

As you know, we see a cross-section of talent. After seeing the first 10 or 15 kids, I begin to realize I'm in for a long day. I know I'm going to hear great songs, like Alicia Keys' "Fallin'" or R. Kelly's "I Believe I Can Fly," being butchered by people who haven't done what I'm telling you to do. (Just trying to keep it real here, guys!)

I sometimes wonder why some of these people punish themselves by coming to the auditions at all. With millions watching, Simon will tell someone trying out, "You're horrible. The worst I ever heard." That person will actually say, "Thank you."

Whoa.

Sometimes I sit there at the judge's table and think, "I'm a part of some wild stuff. This is insanity itself!" What's going on, America? Do we love verbal abuse that much?

As you may know, all kinds of crazy things happen at the auditions. There was a Dallas Cowboys cheerleader who got so excited after her audition that she fell—right under our table. I know you remember her.

We'll see people making fools out of themselves, like the girl who came to see us wrapped in Christmas tree lights and proceeded to plug herself into the wall. Unbelievable. We took one look at her and burst out laughing. You want to be original, but that is going way, way, way beyond originality.

Once in a while we'll get some joker who slips through who just wants to get on TV, like the guy Simon and I dragged out of the judging room during an audition. He was goofing around, making a mockery of the contest. We can spot the pranksters a mile away. We'll say, "Yo, you're not even serious at all. You're just trying to act like a fool." You won't win that way. Ain't no way possible.

But sometimes someone will show up who's really good and I'll go, "Wow. Now this is what I'm here for." Like I said earlier, I usually look for somebody's voice to give me the chills. I'm looking for raw, natural talent, along with a unique sound and a different look. Don't come dressed exactly like Avril or Snoop Dogg or any other star.

Being Idolicious

WHEN JUDGING *IDOL* I LOOK FOR PEOPLE WHO have made a song their own vocally. They don't mimic Nelly Furtado's runs or Justin Timberlake's dance moves. I'm looking for somebody who brings something interesting to the song, like Kelly, Clay, Ruben and Justin did. All the winners have had the ability, the talent and the wherewithal to make that happen.

The funny thing about *Idol* or similar shows is that what we are looking for is the same thing that record labels are looking for, because we on the show all used to work at labels and that's what makes *Idol* tick. Remember, everything in life is relative. I am looking for the same talent I did when I did A&R. You'll hear me say from time to time, "This person has a really good recording voice." Or I'll say, "This is a voice people will believe." That's what it's about.

Truly, we could see 200,000 people per audition and still only find three or four with true potential. That's how tough this is and how long the odds are. Again, anything in life worth having is definitely not going to be free and will definitely cost you some time and effort.

What did successful contestants do right?

THE CRITERIA FOR WINNING ON *IDOL* ARE NO different from the criteria you need to make it at a music label. You still need to become the absolute best that you can be. When setting your course, remember, you are in the Olympics of music, whether you're doing the reality TV show thing or going for a deal. You want to aim for the top. You don't want to be anywhere near the middle or the bottom. And you can do it—if you have "it" and work as hard as you possibly can to get there.

The winners—Kelly, Justin, Ruben and Clay—had almost all of the things that a label looks for, including that uniqueness, "itness" and, of course, hot, hot talent. Almost every successful star on the scene today has those characteristics.

The winners also had conviction. During an audition, it's easy to spot the people who show up with an attitude that says, "I'm not nervous. I'm going to sing my face off. I don't care if there are five people in the room or 55,000. What I do is sing and I'm going to do it like this every time." We saw that in Kelly, Ruben, Clay, Frenchie Davis, Justin and Tamyra, among others.

From day one, these people sounded good. Really good. Some of the audience believed that they got better vocally as the show went on. They were nearly this good the first time we saw them. They started feeling a little more comfortable and had more conviction as the contest progressed. They were, for the most part, consistently good every single time they sang on the show. That's the way you need to be whether it is for a reality TV show or in your career. So if you show up for an audition, be as prepared as you can be.

straight outta da Expert's Mouth

My girl, fellow *American Idol* judge Paula Abdul, can give you her perspective on what it's like to sit at the judge's table and her advice for *Idol*ing and making it in the biz. We have been friends for a very long time and I love working with her.

RANDY: So Paula, we sit next to each other day after day when we're judging *Idol*. We see all kinds of kids—from those who can really sing to those who should have stayed home. What advice do you have for people who think they want to give *American Idol* a shot?

PAULA: I think what we've learned working on the show is that you need to have a sense of reality if you audition. Not just having a healthy ego. I think that's extremely important. I look at some of these kids and say, if I had one-hundredth of the confidence that they have, I would have had such an easier time.

Before you come on the show, do all you can to get a sense of reality about how non-biased people feel about your talent—or lack thereof. Don't just ask your family, who are biased because they love you. Don't ask your best friends, who don't want to hurt your feelings.

Set up rehearsal time and perform for people. Look in the trades or in your local paper and see if there are places where you can perform. If you're still in school, perform in your high school talent show. That will give you a definite dose of reality because it's your peers who are voting for you.

If I'm a big fan of *Idol* and I want to audition, I would try to tape as many shows as possible, especially the early shows, where we focused on pointing out what comes off as farce. Or is just wrong . . . don't do it.

RANDY: What advice do you have for people who want to give the music business a shot?

PAULA: Understand that there is no one way to get in. The beauty of this business is that you can create your own path or blueprint, like I did. I am the master of not conforming to any conventional ways of climbing the ladder to success.

I never thought in a million years that being a Laker Girl would lead me to the career I've had. I knew that I was an accomplished dancer and had the knack for choreography, but I was waiting for the chance to do more. When I got started, I resisted being a Laker Girl, but it was the only outlet I had. So I said, "I'm going to make the best of it. There are famous people who come to see the Los Angeles Lakers play at the Forum and I'm going to create a style of dance that no one's ever seen."

Then I went on to choreograph some of the music industry's biggest-selling artists. I've been nominated and won several Emmys for my choreography on the Academy Awards, *The Tracey Ullman Show* and for the opening number of the American Music Awards. So, then I saved my money up and didn't tell anybody I was making a demo. I ended up landing a deal with Virgin. I had six number-one hits and sold 42 million records. So what I say is follow the path of least resistance. That's what I did.

I bet that if you are trying to make it in the music business, your talents are multifaceted. I got rejections up the wazoo. I would lick my wounds and put my coat of armor on again and go back out there. When a door would shut in my face, I would create different paths for myself. I would go in the back door. Around the side.

Sometimes you have to acknowledge the path of least resistance because that could be the door that opens up and leads you to an amazing career. Sometimes on *Idol*, we see people who have power voices and we tell them they're too theatrical for the competition. Their faces fall. I'll say, "You're young. Have you thought of moving to New York and being on Broadway? You could go to Broadway and have a great career. Look at what someone like Bernadette Peters has done."

I also say to the kids who can sing, but don't feel right for *American Idol*, that this is just one competition. It's a big outlet, but it's just one outlet. So I'll tell them to get back out there. Zero in on the constructive criticism you got and keep going.

Set a time limit for how long you are going to give yourself to make it. Set a five-year limit if you are a teenager and a two-to-three-year limit if you are in your twenties. The reason I say that is because the business has changed and people start much younger now.

Go out there and exhaust every possibility. If after two or three years it's not happening for you, have a backup plan. You may be missing out on being the best doctor, attorney or teacher.

Being tenacious, persistent and being focused and owning the power of knowing what you have are so important. I am living proof of that. When I was getting started, no one helped me. No one in my background helped me.

Since I got started, so many people have said to me, "You'll never be . . . " I've heard that my whole life. People said, "You'll never become a dancer because your legs are too short," or "You are a Laker girl. How do you think you are going to become an industry choreographer?"

Every step of the way of my career there have been major hurdles. I've been told "no" all the way. But I kept going.

And if you've tried everything back home or in the new city you're in, and you're performing in a coffee house or a jazz bar, have fun. Do the best you can. It doesn't mean you can't dream the dream.

And as far as the kids on the show go, you know, Randy, that you and I have a tough time and feel really sad when some of the kids we've watched grow and watched take our constructive criticism and use it to their advantage are eliminated. We know what rejection feels like. I love Simon—the value he brings to the show is the reminder of how difficult this business can be. But, Randy, you and I have both been performers. Simon hasn't. WE know what it feels like to be up there. I think that you would agree, even Simon would have a difficult time facing Simon!

As you all know, Ruben Studdard won the second season of *Idol* with his dope voice. He hit the Top Forty with "Flying Without Wings." He topped the *Billboard* Hot R&B/Hip-Hop Singles Sales chart with "Superstar/Flying Without Wings." He even appeared on the cover of *Rolling Stone*.

RANDY: What advice do you have for people who are coming up in the business?

RUBEN: Stay focused and never let anybody tell you what you can't do. Never lose sight of your dream. But always be realistic.

If you are good at something and you know you are good at something, always continue to do the thing that you're best at and you'll go far.

RANDY: What has been the toughest part of your journey so far?

RUBEN: Just adjusting to my schedule now. Recording an album. Making personal appearances. It's been kind of hectic. There's been a lot of media attention. But the show taught us how to deal with that because they put us in that situation from day one. We had 11 to 12 weeks of media attention. Other than that, the journey has been wonderful and I wouldn't trade it for the world.

RANDY: What advice do you·have for people who want to audition for *Idol*?

RUBEN: The advice I have for people who want to get on a show like *American Idol* is to never take it so seriously, you know? If it's not fun for you, it will show. If you take it too seriously, the slightest disappointment can make you lose sight of what you came there for. Just continue to have a positive attitude and you'll make it.

RANDY: Did you ever think you'd be the last man standing on *Idol*?

RUBEN: I never came on the show trying to win. I actually came just to get the exposure. It's a wonderful venue to get your face and name out there because more than 27 million people watch the show every week.

I just went out and kept having fun and I kept making it farther and farther each week. I put God first with everything I do, so I knew I'd finish with a good outcome.

God is the reason I'm here. I was always excited but never overly surprised. I always did my best. I never left anything out. I'd never go backstage and be like, "Man, I should have sung it like this."

RANDY: What was your most memorable moment on *Idol*?

RUBEN: My most memorable moment was winning. My parents were there. My family was just so excited. I remember seeing my mom cry.

RANDY: How have you been dealing with all of the attention you've gotten since you won?

RUBEN: I'm just having fun. I get a chance to wake up and do a job I love every day. I've been trying to do this my whole life.

I also want to say that Randy, you were a great inspiration for me while I was doing the show and I appreciate how nice you were to me.

RANDY: Thank you, man. I appreciate that.

straight outta da *Expert's Mouth*

Clay Aiken came to see us in *Idol*'s second season and blew us away. After leaving *Idol*, he went on to score a record deal with RCA Records. His first single, "This Is the Night," debuted at number one. His album, *Measure of a Man*, also debuted at number one and went double-platinum in the first week. Way to go, Dawg!

RANDY: You sure don't give up easily. In the show's second season, you first got cut in Charlotte, then you auditioned in Atlanta and won the chance to go onto LA. You made it into the Top 32. The audience voted you off, but then you got another shot as a wild card contestant and came back, yet again, losing to Ruben Studdard by a sliver. How did you keep going through all of this?

CLAY: It was confidence. Believing in yourself and being confident about it and persevering. Really continuing to believe in yourself after you've been told many times that you're not good enough.

When you really feel it and really believe it, then it shows in what you do.

RANDY: Dude, you have taken the world by storm. What advice do you have for kids just starting out?

CLAY: The lesson that I learned the most was about perseverance and really going after something that you want and sticking with it. I got cut twice before I even made it into the Top Ten. It was all about sticking to it. I felt that I had the ability and the talent to go far enough. Farther than I had gotten. So if you feel you have the perseverance and the talent, then go for it.

RANDY: What's been the biggest challenge for you during your *Idol* journey?

CLAY: Balancing the need for competition with the need to still be a friendly peer to everybody on the show was challenging.

I'm not a very competitive person and I had a hard time trying to remember that this was about competition and it was about trying to win. It was about making friends, but it was not just about socializing. I did a good job of convincing myself of that. For the first while, it was not that easy. I think the people who did the best on the show were the people who had the best sense of that—that this is about winning and this is about competing. Yes, I'm going to have fun. Yes, I'm going to make some friends. It's going to be a great experience for me, but I am coming in here with a purpose— to get the job done.

RANDY: What advice do you have for people who want to *Idol*?

CLAY: Be prepared for the attention you may get if you do well on the show. I get stopped in the grocery store and stopped everywhere I go. I can't eat lunch on the patio because people are taking pictures.

I wasn't prepared for everyone else's interest in me. Being able to balance the time that I owe to the public to the time I owe to myself is what I have found most difficult.

RANDY: When you were trying out, did you ever think you'd end up with a record deal and a dope hit song?

CLAY: I dreamed about being in the Top Two and singing in the finale. I didn't look past that. I wanted to win. I felt that I had it in me to win, but I didn't look past winning. I hate to use a cliché, but the saying "Be careful what you wish for" could bite you.

I'm thrilled with all of the success I've had and with all the opportunities I've had. I just want to say to people, and I told this to some of the people on Season 3, that it's not all limos and black-tie affairs. There are some parts that make me question, "Would I like to be a teacher again?" The answer sometimes is yes.

RANDY: What was the most memorable moment of your *Idol* experience?

CLAY: My most memorable experience with *Idol* was going home and singing for my hometown on the tour and coming up on the stage and being introduced for the first time in Raleigh after the show ended.

I come from a medium-sized city that's got a small-town feel to it. The support that came out of that city was unbelievable, unexpected and overwhelming.

One performance can make you . . . or break you

BACK IN CHAPTER 1, I TOLD YOU HOW Tamyra's cold led to her getting booted off the show. Kelly also had a cold that night. They both persevered because they knew they had to go on. But as I said, Tamyra's cold made it harder for her to sing at the level she had been singing at during the contest, which I think affected her psyche. As we all know, that was her last night on the show.

Remember, when you are auditioning, singing, or performing, sometimes you have to overcome all kinds of obstacles. You can never let the way you feel affect your performance, if you can help it. You have to learn to work it out. Hurdles like this will come up in your career many times. Try to stay focused, Dawg.

My most memorable Idolers

I WAS SHOCKED WHEN TAMYRA WAS BOUNCED OUT. She is extremely talented. I think she would have been in the top two if she didn't have such a tough time the night she had a cold.

What's interesting is that she's the kind of artist labels like to sign. She sings amazingly well. She's beautiful. She has charisma. Hollywood has already picked up on that. She appeared on a few episodes of *Boston Public* and is making an album with J Records.

There were quite a few kids I liked on the show —Christopher Aaron, Angela Peel and R.J. Helton in the first season and Kimberly Caldwell, Kimberly Locke and Frenchie Davis in the second.

There are also a few I'll never forget. One of them was Edgar, an Enrique Iglesias wannabe we saw in Miami who didn't even come close. Sure, he dressed like him and warbled an Enrique song. We kept telling him that he didn't have what it takes, but he wouldn't listen. Security guards ended up escorting him out.

Then, when we went to LA, who showed up? Edgar. He put a flip in his hair as if we wouldn't recognize him! But how could we ever forget that voice?

Of course, Keith from Atlanta is one of everybody's all-time favorites. He came in and auditioned for a show that's looking for America's newest superstar. His version of "Like a Virgin" was so hilarious that when he attempted the song, the whole room just roared. No one could believe this kind of sound was humanly possible. We had to take a break for 10 minutes.

So here's what you should learn from this. Yes, seeing a Keith or an Edgar makes it hard to tear your eyes away from the TV. But if you are serious about this business, avoid any delusions at all costs. And if you really are a bad singer, find out *before* you get to a show like *Idol* and spare yourself the ridicule.

Playing the judges

DURING THE AUDITIONS, GUYS OFTEN COME IN AND croon to Paula. They look in her eyes and sing just for her like lovesick puppies, like Simon and I aren't even there. Girls come in and do the same thing to Simon and me. A few brave souls dare to spar with Simon, thinking they'll win him over. (Ha!) Other people come in and perform just for me, like the two of us are down or something.

This is silly. Most people play up to me or Paula because they think we're more sympathetic than Simon. More understanding. My advice? Don't play to anyone. You need to come in and bring it. End of story. You don't need to use any antics—no Christmas tree lights, cartwheels or Rollerblading. This is not the circus. We know what you're doing as soon as you do it.

Whenever anyone plays up to one of the judges, we think they must be kidding. Remember, you have three judges' opinions to deal with and at least two need to be on your side. Don't alienate anybody.

Doing this hurts your chances, unless you really have the goods. But what this says is that you don't believe you have it and deep down you probably know you don't have it. All you've done is make it harder for me to take your talent seriously. I'm apt to be tougher on you if you play up to the judges, as would any judge in any competition.

Ditch the gimmicks

CONTESTANTS BRING US GIFTS. CANDY. ONE PERSON WHO auditioned made hats for us. Others come in with signs or T-shirts bearing our pictures. They try everything to call attention to themselves. This is not what you want to do. None of the winners did this. You want to blow us away with your singing. Impress your talent upon us. That is what we'll remember.

American Idol is one of the country's hottest shows.

We're not fooling around here. We are looking for the next superstar. So if you're deciding to go for the Big Prize on a reality TV show, you have to bring it. The only thing that's going to grab my attention is talent. A great voice and star potential are the only things that will impress me. So if you're coming on the show, good luck.

Yo Dawg: You Just Got Thrown a Bone

CONGRATULATIONS, DUDE. YOU MADE IT THIS FAR THROUGH the music industry maze. Maybe you're one of the lucky few who are in the studio, making your first album. Maybe you're singing backup for Missy Elliott. Or your band is opening for Avril Lavigne.

But maybe you're nowhere near doing any of this. When you tour with your local band, you're staying at the Red Roof Inn instead of the Ritz Carlton. You're driving a beat-up old hooptie instead of a Hummer. You're still delivering Domino's to pay the rent while you chase your dream.

Wherever you are, I'll help you figure out where to go from here, how to keep your wits about you and how to avoid the "charmed goods" that can sideline you for a long time.

But I'm proud of you for gettin' your groove on, keepin'

it moving and goin' for your dream. So here's what I want to say to you: What's up, Dawg! You made it this far!

Record company rhapsody

IF YOU'RE LUCKY ENOUGH TO LAND THAT COVETED record deal, let me be the first to congratulate you. Hopefully, this book has helped you in some way to get it. But as I mentioned in Chapter 7, you have more work to do to keep your career going. You still have to prove yourself. Now you're truly competing with John Mayer, 50 Cent, Pink and all the rest.

Every star I know works harder to stay at the top than they did to get there. You will have to work just as hard as they do. Now that you have the deal, you and your manager, attorney, your band or your musicians, your producers, publisher, songwriters and A&R rep, among others, should all be on the same page, trying to fight the same fight. If not, you have to do what I told you earlier. Cut bait and move on. Find new people if members of your team ain't doin' it for you.

You and your team must figure out how you or your band can go on to become a bigger success. Success, to me, is not about money. It's about loving what you do and being the best you can be at it.

But in the music business, success is based on the bottom line. How many records you've sold. How much money you're raking in for the company. I'm going to be one of the only ones to tell you that you don't need to be an overnight success to have a long, fruitful career. If you sell 400,000 or

500,000 records your first time out, good for you, Dawg. The company won't make tons of money and nobody will be jumping up and down but it's a respectable start.

And you want to keep it going. This is about you building your mountain. You don't want to build a little molehill and have people say, "Okay, next."

I know it's hard, but you gotta be patient

ONCE YOU LAND A DEAL, YOU'RE PROBABLY GOING to want everything right away. The money. The bling. The all-out media blitz. The crazed fans. The dudes or the chicks. But you really don't. When a breakout star sells 10 million copies of his or her first record and sweeps the Grammys, it's sometimes considered the kiss of death. Why? If you get it all at once, it means there is nowhere else to go. It's harder than ever to top what you've already done. And when fame comes on too strong, it can be pretty hard to handle. You want to continue to grow. You want to take it slow.

Just a bit more about your first album

YOUR MANAGER, PRODUCER, LAWYER AND ALL THE PEOPLE at the label saw your talent and your "itness." They believe in you. Now you need to prove that to the public.

The album you are about to make is the most important calling card you now have. When your music is played on KIIS-FM in LA or The Beat or some other radio station, you want somebody to pull the car over and go, "Who the hell is this? I've got to find out." If people aren't touched by your music, you've got a problem.

You want to move people with your music. You want to have them get up and dance. If you're doing hip-hop, you want to have people excited enough to learn the lines, like the lyrics in 50 Cent's song "21 Questions." These are lyrics you've never heard anybody say. They stick with you. They make you smile.

So you have to keep doing what I told you at the beginning of this book: setting short- and long-term goals to keep the momentum going. You're building a career. If you want to be a flash-in-the-pan, or a one-hit wonder, then you can sign on the dotted line, but don't cry when it ends just when it got started.

You want to try and develop a respectable career, like Mariah Carey, Missy Elliott, Coldplay, Red Hot Chili Peppers, Outkast, Jay-Z, Dr. Dre, Sum 41, Whitney Houston, Faith Hill, Celine Dion, No Doubt, and the rest of the A-listers I've been talking about in this book.

Reinventing yourself

I'VE BEEN PLAYING BASS SINCE I WAS A kid. But just last week, I was saying to myself that I'm going to start practicing bass two hours a day, if I can. I discovered something new that I'm dying to work on. Something else I think I can bring to my playing.

Reinvention is king. The reason a band like the Rolling Stones has been around for so long is because they know how to keep reinventing themselves. Reinvention doesn't mean just completely changing who you are. It's coming at something from a different angle, to keep people interested. It could mean practicing more, trying out something new, failing sometimes but always trying again. This is another way you can keep your career moving.

Still in the trenches

SO YOU DIDN'T GET THE ELUSIVE RECORD DEAL yet. You didn't make it onto a reality TV show like *American Idol*. You're not singing backup for Madonna. Nothing has locked yet.

Stay the course if this is what you really are trying to achieve in your life. Keep practicing, learning, networking and trying to make everything come together. As I've said in this book, making it in the music business is one of the hardest journeys on the planet. It can take a very long time to get where you want to go. You think five years is a long time to shop a demo? Dude, that's nothing.

If it makes you feel better, you're in good company. Almost all of the people you hear on the radio, see on MTV or BET or whose records you buy at the Virgin Megastore or Tower Records worked this hard to get where they are. If you stay on it, eventually your day will come and you will get your shot. Don't give up the fight if you've come this far and you've worked this hard.

As I've said in previous chapters, if you've lost your way or you're confused about where you are on your journey, retrace your steps. I want to know that you're giving this your best shot. Go over everything until you get it right. Try things from a different angle. Get fresh opinions.

But remember what I told you at the beginning of this book. You need to have "it" or some kind of "itness" to make RCA, Def Jam, Virgin, Warner Brothers or Interscope or any of the other companies want to sign you. You have to be dope enough to compete with Good Charlotte, Radiohead and Nelly and everyone else who's on the radio and selling millions of records. Is your song as good as Limp Bizkit's? Ja Rule's? Eminem's?

straight outta da Expert's Mouth

Like you, there are lots of people out there who are trying to make it. As I've told you, it's not easy out there, but if you persist and if you have talent, you can get yourself on the road to success.

Shalonda Wilson grew up in Grand Rapids, Michigan, and started singing at family functions when she was in elementary school. When she graduated from high school, she auditioned for the band where her father played the saxophone and began her career.

RANDY: So you've been working at this for the past 13 years. What's your journey been like?

SHALONDA: After singing on the live, local circuit for a few years, I moved to New York for a year in 1995 to pursue a singing career. I had a demo deal with Sony/Columbia. They were looking at me as an artist and paid for me to complete a demo, but nothing came of it.

I went on to pursue a gospel deal in New York, but the label closed. So I moved back to Grand Rapids and got back on the local scene, singing R&B, gospel, jazz and blues. I gained a local following doing my thing with a band. I started a booking agency, booking other musicians, and started a Wednesday night club night where I could perform and showcase other local talent as well.

In 2002, I moved to LA. I figured that there were more opportunities there. I quit my job working for the city of Grand Rapids making and installing traffic signs. That was my day job. At night I was performing.

You have to have a day job. That's your reality check. That keeps you grounded.

Moving to LA was a huge risk. But after being in LA for two weeks, I got my first job singing background for Monica on Jay Leno.

RANDY: How did you get your first job so fast?

SHALONDA: I was picking up a friend who was doing some work at a company in Los Angeles. He does work for a number of companies, so I didn't know where he was working that particular night. My friend was getting off work late and while I waited for him, I realized that I was in the offices of activentertainment, a talent agency. I seized the opportunity and ended up auditioning for the owner, Bruce Sterling, that night.

Bruce liked me and got me my first gig. I've been working ever since. The first tour I did was with Tony award-winner

Heather Headley, who starred in the original production of *Aida*. I still sing for her.

I also sang backup for Kelly Clarkson when she was on Jay Leno and the *Today* show, I sang backup for Shaggy when he was on Jay Leno and I did a couple theater shows with Ziggy Marley. I've done a few dates with Mya and sang backup for Clay Aiken when he did Jay Leno and a string of other shows.

RANDY: What is your advice for people just starting out?

SHALONDA: If they're anything like me, never give up. I would recommend that people work on their craft. You can work on your craft right where you are, whether it's Grand Rapids, Michigan, or Los Angeles, California. I think it was part of God's plan to send me home in '95 to work on my craft. I went home and got a whole lot of things crackin' to bring me up to a more professional level. That's why I believe I'm more prepared the second time around. Hone your skills, perfect your craft and go for it, but make sure you're ready when you hit the big leagues.

RANDY: Why haven't you given up yet?

SHALONDA: This is something that I've always wanted to do since I was a little girl. My passion and drive are so incredible. But it's not an easy thing to do. It's a scrape-and-struggle kind of industry.

You may want to hang back for now

MAYBE YOU'RE PRETTY GOOD BUT DON'T THINK YOU have what it takes to land a major deal. You don't have to give up music altogether. Nothing says that if you don't have a record deal you're not successful.

You could still make a great living as a working musician until you get yourself together and want to try it all again, which is what a lot of up-and-comers do. You could still play those local gigs. You could make some cheddar playing weddings and parties. You can play clubs in a Top Forty cover band. You could do dinner theater, Off-Broadway or maybe even Broadway. You could sing back-up for smaller acts. You could pursue another career and play or sing on the side.

Should you use it or lose it?

IF PROS YOU TRUST HAVE TOLD YOU REPEATEDLY that they like you, think you're nice, smart, cute, or whatever, but that you absolutely, positively DO NOT have what it takes to make it big and never will—and you know, deep in your heart, that you really don't have what it takes—then you may want to do something else. If this sounds like you, then let it go. You know who you are. Yo, say goodnight. Give yourself the time to find out what it is you are meant to do. Research the possibilities and go for it.

straight outta da Dawg's Mouth—*tip 18*

If you do decide to stay in the game, please don't let money be your motivator. Do this because you love it. Because you know deep in your heart that you have talent. Don't do it because you want fast money, because the money ain't gonna be fast, trust me. This is too hard of a business.

As I said, the road will be lined with obstacles, so you must have an unbelievable love of music to sustain you. When I was getting started, I put music first in my life almost before everything else, right after God and family, especially that summer when I immersed myself in playing and learning everything I could about the bass. I really gave myself fully to trying to get my chops together musically because I knew that if I really gave myself to the music, I would get a 100 percent return from it. And that's what carried me through my career to where I am today.

Don't be too obsessed, though

IN THIS BOOK, I'VE TOLD YOU TO PRACTICE as much as you can, try to land as many gigs as possible, play as many shows as possible, take classes, network, all while possibly holding down a day job. So, you wonder, how does that leave time for anything else?

You have to learn how to balance everything. Even though your plate will be full, you shouldn't neglect your family, friends, or your health on your grueling way to the top. You've got to learn to set priorities because everything in life is relative. If one thing is off balance, everything will be off balance.

You need your family and friends in your support system. You also need to nurture them at the same time. You want them to be proud that they were there on your way up.

The wannabes can't wait to live in the big houses with the glitz, the glamour, the clothes and the cars. If you've alienated your family and friends, no matter how much stuff you have, you're going to see how empty it can be without them. As they say, it can be pretty lonely at the top. So take some time for your family and friends. E'rybody needs love, yo.

Psychologically speaking

IF YOU HAVE AN ADDICTIVE PERSONALITY, BE ULTRA-careful. In this business, people will be partying everywhere you go. Please stay away from what I call the charmed goods, like drinking, drugs and whatever else takes you away from getting the job done. All of these vices can pull you under before you even get your career started. They can also end your career.

Some people want to escape their reality. Don't be those people. You want to live in reality. Reality is what's going to help you get where you want to go, not a false sense of euphoria for 15 minutes.

You might say, "Come on. How could a little partying hurt?" Yo, it will take you off your path so fast. It will distract you. It will interrupt your life. If you are serious about making it in this business, don't even go there. You've seen it happen to so many stars that you know and admire.

If you're unhappy in your life or have been sidetracked by an addiction, please seek psychological help or counseling to help you work things out.

To calm your nerves, you can try meditation, yoga or exercising. Turn to your church, synagogue or any other kind of spiritual enlightenment. Talk to a good friend to help you through it. This is your journey. You're trying to stay on your path and figure out what's best for you.

So, be most careful. And true, true, true. Please seek professional help and guidance if you feel like you're falling off the path or if you feel that the way you're living your life is taking you away from your dream—and everything else.

Other obstacles

WATCH OUT FOR ALL THE FAIR-WEATHER FRIENDS who may come your way. Don't let people take advantage of you. The higher you go in this business, the more competitive it becomes. Jealousy, envy, back-stabbing can all come into play. Some people may say they want to partner up with you or help you out as a friend, when all the while, they're trying to take you down. Remember, everybody wants to win. Everyone is after the Holy Grail.

With experience, you'll be able to spot these people easily. Follow your heart and intuition. If you feel like people are being snaky, lose them. You only want to surround yourself with winners and sponge and learn from their wisdom. You want to get away from the people who are trying to bring you down.

Don't kid yourself

I'M GOING TO SHARE SOME TRUTHS AND MYTHS about the business that you should keep in the back of your mind as you continue your journey:

■ **MYTH:** I'm an OK singer, but I'm as gorgeous as Beyoncé. Clive Davis should be calling any day now.

■ **TRUTH:** Being cute, sexy, a good dancer, a dope dresser or class clown at school does not mean you have "it" to be a singer or musician. Because you have the drive, determination and confidence does not mean that you have "it." Working hard and staying focused will help you fine-tune the "itness" you have and help take you to the top.

• • •

■ **MYTH:** I only just started taking lessons. My teacher can't believe how fast I've progressed. I'm a natural. I must be ready for a record deal.

■ **TRUTH:** You might be a natural. You might be really good. But you just started. If you're really that talented, you may be ready sooner than most, but it will still take you a while to get off the ground. You still have a lot of work to do.

■ **MYTH:** I was at the mall the other day and guess who I saw? Gwen Stefani! I dropped my bags and started singing, right there in front of Rampage! She told me I have a great voice. If someone like Gwen says I'm good, I know that I'm ready for the big time!

■ **TRUTH:** Wait a minute. If somebody famous or otherwise tells you that you are talented, you have to ask yourself, are you that good or was that person just being nice? Do you really have "it"? Do you have a hit song? Have you been working and practicing every minute you can? You have to make sure you are as dope as people are telling you before you go for that record deal. Don't be delusional.

· · ·

■ **MYTH:** People in the club where I play every weekend tell me I'm the best rapper they ever heard. Dr. Dre is going to have me on speed dial soon.

■ **TRUTH:** Just because people ask you for your autograph in the one club where you play doesn't mean you're ready for the world yet. It means the people in that club like you. When you have fans lining up for tickets to your shows weeks in advance, then you might be on your way.

· · ·

■ **MYTH:** My friends and family say I'm the best singer they ever heard. My mom swears that I'm better than Nelly Furtado. My dad is so proud of me that he cries when I sing. (You sure he's not in pain? Just kidding!) Everyone keeps telling me to keep trying out for these big auditions. If they're all saying this, I must be ready.

■ **TRUTH:** It's good to have confidence, but watch that you don't go overboard with it. Your friends and family may convince you that you are ready, but only you and your teacher can decide that. You want to keep it real now and throughout your career.

• • •

■ **MYTH:** People say I sing like Christina Aguilera, so now I'm gonna start looking like her, too. I'm going to dye my hair and wear tons of makeup, just like she does, so people will mistake me for her. That way, I'll make it.

■ **TRUTH:** Copying someone's look and voice will ensure one thing: that you won't make it. Shows like *Idol* and recording companies look for originality and talent. Learn from others but don't emulate them. You'll never be as good as the original. You want to be you.

• • •

■ **MYTH:** A producer I just met says he'll record all my songs for free. But he wants me to come to the studio from 2 A.M. to 6 A.M.

■ **TRUTH:** Not many people start recording sessions at 2. This producer may want you there at 2 because he wants to get busy with you. If it doesn't sound right to you, don't do it. Please be careful out there!

• • •

■ **MYTH:** A manager says, "Sign with me. I've got this contract for five years. You don't need an attorney because we gotta do this fast. Just sign it."

■ **TRUTH:** Run. Somebody's trying to pull a fast one on you. You need a reputable attorney to look over every document that comes your way. Never sign anything without consulting with your lawyer first.

• • •

■ **MYTH:** A producer says, "I have a one-page contract for you. It's really simple. Take it home and look it over."

■ **TRUTH:** Tear it up. Nothing is ever that simple when you are signing a contract.

• • •

■ **MYTH:** I've read every book and magazine about the business. I know what contracts are. I know what points are. I know everything there is to know. I could negotiate anything for myself. I don't need a lawyer or a manager.

■ **TRUTH:** Are you crazy? It's good to understand the business so you don't get taken, but you need professionals to help guide you when making deals and signing contracts.

• • •

■ **MYTH:** Three labels want to sign you. One of the companies says they'll give you final approval on everything from the producers for the album to the artwork for the CD cover. You'll have total control.

■ **TRUTH:** Sometimes labels promise you the world just to get you to sign with them. As soon as they clinch the deal, half of that could go away. Make sure you get everything in writing before you sign on the dotted line and that your lawyer has thoroughly read the fine print.

• • •

■ **MYTH:** A producer keeps coming to your show. He wants to sign you. It's the only lead you have right now. But you've heard shaky things about him and his company. But you think, "I may as well go for it because I have nothing else going on. I may not get another offer like this."

■ **TRUTH:** Sometimes not doing anything is better than doing something that could potentially tie you up for a long time and hurt your career. If you've researched the company's background and don't like what you've learned, steer clear. Look for other opportunities.

• • •

■ **MYTH:** A production company that specializes in TV wants to make you their first musical act. They want to help you develop your alternative band. You're thinking, "Wow. Of all the acts, they chose mine to do first. I'll do it."

■ **TRUTH:** If this company specializes in TV, that's what they're good at. The music business is a sexy industry. Everyone wants to be a part of it. Don't be the first act they develop. Wait to see how well they do with other acts before you sign up.

MYTH: A shady character has been hanging out at the club saying he can bankroll you and help put you in the game. No strings attached.

TRUTH: What are you thinking? Of course there are strings attached! Stay away.

. . .

MYTH: My demo has been rejected 10 times by various labels. My teacher says I have no talent. But I think I do. Maybe I should try out for a show like *Idol*. It can't be that hard to win.

TRUTH: Next.

. . .

MYTH: You decide you are going to come to an *Idol* audition dressed as SpongeBob SquarePants with the tail of a zebra. You are going to hand out the Crabby Patties that SpongeBob likes to eat so the judges will remember you.

TRUTH: You are right. We will never forget you, but you probably won't make it on a show like *Idol* in a get-up like that. We are looking for the best talent, only.

. . .

MYTH: You won in a beauty pageant and now you want to audition for *Idol*. You warbled Frank Sinatra's "My Way" during the pageant's talent competition. You definitely didn't win because of your singing.

TRUTH: You are probably beautiful but don't sing that

well. There's beauty pageant singing, theatrical singing and competitive, recording artist singing. No matter what you think, we'll still tell you that you are a beauty pageant singer. We'll see right through it.

· · ·

■ **MYTH:** I've been taking lessons for 10 years. My teacher says I'm getting stronger. I haven't been able to get any gigs yet. It's going to happen for me soon.

■ **TRUTH:** The teacher is lying to you and you are lying to yourself. Get out now.

So think these things through and don't let them happen to you!

Signing off

I WANTED TO WRITE THIS BOOK TO TRY and enlighten you, because, yo, man, so many people have helped me on my journey. God knows I didn't make it by myself and I doubt that you will either. You need people to help you on your road to the top.

I hope that some of what I've told you in this book has inspired you and taught you some helpful things about this magical mystery tour you're undertaking.

Writing this book is one of my ways of giving back to a profession that has been so amazingly great for me. I can't even begin to count the ways that I have benefited from making music my life.

I hope you, too, enjoy the riches that a love of music can bring. Dude, I hope you make it. I want you to make it. I want you to be successful.

Peace, love and wisdom.

Randy Jackson

Suggested Listening

THIS IS JUST A BRIEF LIST OF ARTISTS, producers and songwriters that you should be familiar with if you are going to work in the music business.

Aretha Franklin

James Brown

Bill Withers

Marvin Gaye

The Temptations

The Four Tops

The O'Jays

The Supremes

Stevie Wonder

Rufus and Chaka Kahn

Frankie Beverly and Maze

Billy Paul

Minnie Ripperton

Roger and Zapp

The Ohio Players

New Birth

War

Shirley Murdock

Candi Staton

Ann Peebles

Johnny Taylor

The Isley Brothers

Michael McDonald

The Righteous Brothers

Olivia Newton John

Michael Jackson

Janet Jackson

The Jackson Five

Luther Vandross

Smokie Norful

The Funky Meters

Tyrone Davis

Kirk Franklin

Donny McKlurkin

Howlin' Wolf

Bessie Smith

Dinah Washington

Anita Baker

Earth, Wind and Fire

Dionne Warwick

Patti LaBelle

Gladys Knight and
the Pips

Sam Cooke

B.B. King

Robert Johnson

Muddy Waters

Lightning Hopkins

Taj Mahal

Etta James

John Lee Hooker

Slim Harpo

Albert King

Freddie King

Albert Collins

Thelonious Monk

Charlie Parker

Sarah Vaughan

Ella Fitzgerald

Herbie Hancock

John McLaughlin and
the Mahavishnu
Orchestra

Brecker Brothers

Clifford Brown

Jaco Pastorius

Miles Davis

Billie Holiday

The Everly Brothers

The Whispers

Jeff Buckley

Elvis Presley

Tony Bennett

Ray Charles

Nat King Cole

Frank Sinatra

Sammy Davis Jr.

Chet Baker

Fats Domino

Chubby Checker

Edgar and Johnny
Winter

Grand Central Station

The Commodores

The Mamas and
the Papas

J. Geils

Carole King

The Gap Band

Al Garrone

Count Basie

The Brothers Johnson

James Cotton

Reverend Al Green

Todd Rundgren

Phili International

Teddy Pendergrass

Waylon Jennings

BeBe and CeCe
Winans and family

Edwin and Walter
Hawkins

Ann Nesby

Shirley Caesar

Sounds of Blackness

Kim Burrell

The Clark Sisters

Fred Hammond

Commissioned

Mozart

Bach

Beethoven

Brahms

Vivaldi (The Four
Seasons)

Joni Mitchell

Cat Stevens

James Taylor

Lester Flatt and Earl
Scruggs

Iggy Pop

Paul Simon

Simon and Garfunkel

Peter Gabriel

Robert Palmer

Bob Seger

Luis Miguel

Rod Stewart

Lionel Ritchie

Prince

The Time

The Eurythmics

Duran Duran

Abba

The Steve Miller Band

Jefferson Airplane

Yes

Boston

Stevie Ray Vaughan

Neil Young

ZZ Top

Aerosmith

Black Sabbath

Def Leppard

The Clash

Foreigner

David Bowie

Led Zeppelin

The Eagles

Queen

Journey

The Rolling Stones

The Beatles

Cream

Jimi Hendrix

Janis Joplin

Elton John

Fleetwood Mac

U2

Bob Dylan

AC/DC

The Police

Bruce Springsteen

Van Halen

Genesis

Doobie Brothers

Billy Joel

Chicago

Santana

The Talking Heads

Bon Jovi

Pat Benatar

Joan Jett

The Cars

Bee Gees

The Allman Brothers

Blood, Sweat and Tears

Parliament

P-Funk All Stars

Funkadelic

Sly and the Family Stone

George Clinton

Tower of Power

Hank Williams Sr.

Willie Nelson

Johnny Cash	Tony Toni Tone
Faith Hill	The Roots
The Judds	P. Diddy
The Grateful Dead	Eminem
Kansas	Dr. Dre
Kenny Loggins	Snoop Dogg
Dixie Chicks	Missy Elliott
Alan Jackson	Da Brat
Martina McBride	Outkast
Keith Urban	De La Soul
George Strait	Busta Rhymes
Brooks & Dunn	Tupac
Alabama	Biggie Smalls
Garth Brooks	Jay-Z
Shania Twain	Ice Cube
Vince Gill	N.W.A.
The Soggy Bottom Boys	Beastie Boys
Brad Paisley	Mos Def
James Ingram	Run-D.M.C.
Bobby McFerrin	A Tribe Called Quest
Jimmy Cliff	The Pharcyde
Peter Tosh	Talib Kweli
Bob Marley	Nelly
New Edition	Ludacris
Bobby Brown	50 Cent
Take 6	LL Cool J
Jodeci	Arrested Development

TLC

The Fugees

Lauryn Hill

Mary J. Blige

Erykah Badu

Beyoncé Knowles

Destiny's Child

Britney Spears

Christina Aguilera

*NSYNC

Backstreet Boys

Justin Timberlake

Madonna

Celine Dion

Whitney Houston

Seal

Sheryl Crow

Tori Amos

Norah Jones

Beck

No Doubt

John Mayer

Van Hunt

Nikka Costa

Dionne Farris

Dave Matthews Band

The Cult

Jane's Addiction

Metallica

Radiohead

Coldplay

Nirvana

Foo Fighters

Maroon 5

Red Hot Chili Peppers

Korn

Limp Bizkit

Linkin Park

Guns N' Roses

Sonic Youth

Stone Temple Pilots

Master P

Rage Against the Machine

Alice in Chains

Pink Floyd

Green Day

Sex Pistols

Tool

Mudvayne

Pearl Jam

Soundgarden

Primus

ARTISTS/SONGWRITERS/
PRODUCERS

Neil Sedaka

Trevor Horn

Timbaland

The Neptunes

LA Reid and Babyface

Burt Bacharach and
Hal David

Diane Warren

Thom Bell and Linda
Creed

Holland-Dozier-Holland

Jimmy Jam & Terry
Lewis

Jermaine Dupri

David Kahne

Butch Vig

Philidelphia
International

Andy Wallace

Gil Norton

Mark "Spike" Stent

Natalie Hooker

Kanye West

Just Blaze

Brendan O'Brien

GG Garth

Acknowledgments

I WOULD LIKE TO THANK THE FOLLOWING PEOPLE who have touched my life in many amazing ways. I don't know where in the world I would be if you hadn't graced my life. You've given me your wisdom, guidance, help and experience that have been so valuable for me in developing my career. I can never thank you enough. The list is in no particular order. If I forget anyone, just know it's not because I don't appreciate you. I have nothing but love for your support and help along the way.

K. C. Baker

Paula Balzer

Bob Miller

Gretchen Young

Hyperion Books

Ralph Rubenstein

Julia D. Jackson

Herman C. Jackson Sr.

Herman C. Jackson Jr.

Erika Jackson

Taylor Jackson

Liz Jackson

Zoe Jackson

Jordan Jackson

The extended Jackson family

Sue Ann Lewis

Wendy Nicole Wiggins

Sue Ann Dangerfield

Sammy Thornton

Big Bo Melvin and The Nitehawks

Tiny Tim

Ted Cosey

Slim Harpo

John Ivey

Ron Anderson

Judy Stakee

Bob Johnson

Buddy Stewart

John Landau

Clarence Clemons

Alvin Batiste

Steve Perry

Neal Schon

Steve Smith

Jonathan Cain

Ross Valory

Journey

John Fred & The Playboys

Jon Bon Jovi

Richie Sambora

Bob Dylan

Bruce Springsteen

Billy Joel

Mariah Carey

Whitney Houston

Celine Dion

Keith Richards

Steve Jordan

Charlie Drayton

Waddy Wachtel

Don Henley

Danny Korthman

Narada Michael Walden

David Rubinson

Tom Coster

Carlos Santana

Billy Cobham

Jean-Luc Ponty

Herbie Hancock

Chuck Rainey

Sterling Ball—Music Man Guitars

Mike Connoly

Jack Wilson

Corrado Rustici

Zucherro Vasco Rossi

Mike Darnell/Fox

Gail Berman/Fox

Sandy Grushow/Fox

Randy Civello

Roy Ahbert

Dr. Valerin Smith

Johnnie Gerbrecht

Elvin Noiseworthy

Woofy

Reverend E. J. Ford

Vinnie Calaiuta

Steve Lukather

Eddie Van Halen

The late Jeff Picaro

Hot Ice

Black Blood & the
Chocolate Pickles

Lynn Orso

Bill Carter

Phil Kaffel

Richie Zito

Marty Cohen

Tommy Mottola

Donny Inner

Roy Bittan

Jay Boberg

Barry Gibb

Tom Dowd

Jeffery Nead

Simon Cowell

Paula Abdul

Ryan Seacrest

Nigel Lythgoe

Ken Warrick

Simon Fuller

Kelly Clarkson

Ruben Studdard

Justin Guarini

Clay Aiken

John Stevens

Peter Karpin

Dennis Handlin

Kenny MacPherson

Jeff Frasco/CAA

Michael Katcher/CAA

Rob Light/CAA

Elie Dekel/CAA

Mark Stroud

Kevin Liles

Jeff Fenster

Lyor Cohen

Irving Rubenstein

Orite Levy

J. Mitchel

Lionel Cole

Kevin Guarneri

MCA Records

Columbia Records

Andy Slater

Matt and Dean Serletic

Roy Lott

Barry Squire

Benny Medina

Johnny Wright

L. Lee Phillips

Bruce Flohr

Liz Rosenberg

Shalonda Wilson

Ron Rutlidge and the Henson Recording Studio family

Charity Lomax and the Westlake Recording Studio family

Mark Bess

Ruby Azrach

Norman Weissfeld

The Malouf Brothers

Lionel Ritchie

The Divinyls

John Coltrane

Michael Mauldin

Jermaine Dupri

Jimmy Jam and Terry Lewis

Branford Marsalis

Taxxi (the Band)

Tamyra Gray

Kimberly Caldwell

Diane Warren

Aretha Franklin

Frankie Beverly

Gerald Busby

Steve Corbin

Don Was

Will Botwin

John Weakland

Bobby Stevens

Penny Ford

Nikka Costa

Justin Stanley

Stephen Bray (Breakfast Club—the band)

Pat Leonard

Henry Butler

Ernie K-Do

Clarence Gatemouth Brown

Syl Johnson

O. V. Wright

Eric Daniels

Vernon "Ice" Black

Gigi Gonaway

Bruce Sterling

Maneca Lightner

Irving Azoff

Matthew Knowles

Destiny's Child

Van Hunt

Dionne Farris

Avant

Steve Huff

Eric Patton

Buck Richardson's
Night Club in Clinton,
Louisiana

Greg Digiovine

Clive Davis

Louise McNally

Eddie Money

Lee Parvin

Kenny Gill

Woodrow Barnes

John Smith

Sweet Pepper
(the Band)

Clarence Render

Larry Seibert

Charles Goldstruck

Jeff Redd

Benny Medina

David Kahne

Don Henley

Gemma Corfield

Jeremy Lasalle

Linda Blum

Penny Ford

Marla McNally

Don Passman

Helen Stotler

Henry Root

Fred Davis

Bootsy Collins

Grover Jackson

Jimmy Hester

James Jameison

Larry Grahm

Jaco Pastorius

Kenny Loggins

Madonna

David Foster

Stanley Clark

Jimi Hendrix

Greg Wright

Steve Moir

Jimmy Iovine

Tracy Chapman

John Fogerty

Sly Stone

Loretta Baker

Beyoncé Knowles

Kim Burse

David Ryan Harris

Peavey Electronics

Ibanez Guitars

Dean Markley

Line 6

SWR

Mike Lull Guitars

Yamaha—Chris & Tara

All the clubs, bars, weddings, parties etc. . . . that I ever played at.